185 Bodybuilding Meal and Shake Recipes to Make You Look Incredible

Create a sculpted and ripped body in half the time!

By

Joseph Correa

Certified Sports Nutritionist

COPYRIGHT

© 2016 Finibi Inc

All rights reserved

Reproduction or translation of any part of this work beyond that permitted by section 107 or 108 of the 1976 United States Copyright Act without the permission of the copyright owner is unlawful.

This publication is designed to provide accurate and authoritative information in regard to the subject matter covered. It is sold with the understanding that neither the author nor the publisher is engaged in rendering medical advice. If medical advice or assistance is needed, consult with a doctor. This book is considered a guide and should not be used in any way detrimental to your health. Consult with a physician before starting this nutritional plan to make sure it's right for you.

ACKNOWLEDGEMENTS

The realization of this book could not have been possible without the support and motivation of my family.

185 Bodybuilding Meal and Shake Recipes to Make You Look Incredible

Create a sculpted and ripped body in half the time!

By

Joseph Correa

Certified Sports Nutritionist

CONTENTS

Copyright

Acknowledgements

About The Author

Introduction

Bodybuilding Calendar

Bodybuilding Meal Recipes

Bodybuilding Shake Recipes

Fat Reducing Calendar

Fat Reducing Meal Recipes

Fat Reducing Juice Recipes

Other Great Titles by This Author

ABOUT THE AUTHOR

As a certified sports nutritionist and professional athlete, I firmly believe that proper nutrition will help you reach your goals faster and effectively. My knowledge and experience has helped me live healthier throughout the years and which I have shared with family and friends. The more you know about eating and drinking healthier, the sooner you will want to change your life and eating habits.

Being successful in controlling your weight is important as it will improve all aspects of your life.

Nutrition is a key part in the process of getting in better shape and that's what this book is all about.

INTRODUCTION

185 Bodybuilding Meal and Shake Recipes to Make You Look Incredible will help you pack lots of protein in your diet and reduce your fat intake to create a ripped and sculpted body. The meal and shake recipes, along with the calendar, will help you increase muscle mass and cut fat in an accelerated and organized manner so that you can schedule what you eat and when.

Make sure you know what you're eating by preparing it yourself or having someone prepare it for you.

This book will help you to:

-Increase muscle mass to look bigger and stronger.

- Drop excess fat in your body.

-Have more energy during training.

-Naturally accelerate Your Metabolism.

-Improve how you look and how you feel.

Joseph Correa is a certified sports nutritionist and a professional athlete.

BODYBUILDING CALENDAR

Week 1

Day 1:

Early Riser Breakfast

Snack: Blueberry Yogurt

Tuna Burger and Salad

Snack: Cherry Tomatoes with Cottage Cheese

Mexican Style Protein Bowl

Day 2:

Blueberry Lemon Pancakes

Snack: Avocado on Toast

Spicy Beefsteak Kebabs

Snack: Apple and Peanut Butter

Mediterranean Fish

Day 3:

Power Bowl

Snack: Yogurt with Tropical Fruit

Stuffed Chicken Breast with Brown Rice

Snack: Bell Pepper with Cottage Cheese

Vegan Friendly Dinner

Day 4:

Almond Milk Smoothie

Snack: Cup of Popcorn

Pancetta-wrapped Pollock with Potatoes

Snack: Yogurt with Dried Goji Berries

Garlicky Hummus

Day 5

Greek Yogurt with Flaxseeds and Apple

Snack: Rice Cake with Peanut Butter

Baked Salmon with Grilled Asparagus

Snack: Celery Sticks with Goat Cheese and Green Olives

Chicken with Avocado Salad

Day 6:

Breakfast 'Pizza'

Snack: Greek Yogurt with Strawberries

Chicken Caesar Wraps

Snack: Roasted Chickpeas

Hot Cod

Day 7:

Bell Pepper Rings with 'Frit Grits'

Snack: Nut Mix

Beef and Broccoli Noodles

Snack: Ham and Celery Sticks

Arugula Chicken Salad

Week 2

Day 1:

Whey Protein Muffins

Snack: Avocado on Toast

Shrimp and Zucchini Linguine Pasta Salad

Snack: Apple and Peanut Butter

Tofu Burger

Day 2:

Mexican Mocha Breakfast

Snack: Yogurt with Dried Goji Berries

Trout with Potato Salad

Snack: Cup of Popcorn

Chicken with Pineapple and Bell Peppers

Day 3:

Smoked Salmon and Avocado with Toast

Snack: Cherry Tomatoes with Cottage Cheese

Spiced Chicken

Snack: Blueberry Yogurt

Grilled Mushroom and Zucchini Burger

Day 4:

Fruit and Peanut Butter Smoothie

Snack: Roasted Chickpeas

Mexican Bean Chili

Snack: Greek Yogurt with Strawberries

Sweet and Sour Chicken

Day 5:

Protein-packed Scramble

Snack: Bell pepper with Cottage Cheese

Turkey Meatloaf with Whole Wheat Couscous

Snack: Yogurt with Tropical Fruit

Dijon Mustard Halibut

Day 6:

Pumpkin Pie Protein Pancakes

Snack: Ham and Celery Sticks

Mediterranean Rice

Snack: Nut Mix

Tuna Melt

Day 7:

Tuna Stuffed Bell Peppers

Snack: Celery Sticks with Goat Cheese and Green Olives

Beef Meatball Pasta with Spinach

Snack: Rice Cake with Peanut Butter

Sushi Bowl

Week 3

Day 1:

High-protein Oatmeal

Snack: Cup of Popcorn

Stuffed Eggs with Pita Bread

Snack: Apple and Peanut Butter

Tray Bake Chicken

Day 2:

Early Riser Breakfast

Snack: Avocado on Toast

Beef and Broccoli Noodles

Snack: Yogurt with Dried Goji Berries

Garlicky Hummus

Day 3:

Power Bow

Snack: Greek Yogurt with Strawberries

Chicken Caesar Wraps

Snack: Cherry Tomatoes with Goat Cheese

Mediterranean Fish

Day 4:

Blueberry Lemon Pancakes

Snack: Roasted Chickpeas

Baked Salmon with Grilled Asparagus

Snack: Blueberry Yogurt

Arugula Chicken Salad

Day 5:

Greek Yogurt with Flaxseeds and Apple

Snack: Ham and Celery Sticks

Tuna Burger and Salad

Snack: Yogurt with Tropical Fruit

Chicken with Avocado Salad

Day 6:

Bell Pepper Rings with 'Frit Grits'

Snack: Bell Peppers with Cottage Cheese

Stuffed Chicken Breast with Brown Rice

Snack: Nut Mix

185 Bodybuilding Meal and Shake Recipes to Make You Look Incredible

Hot Cod

Day 7:

Almond Milk Smoothie

Snack: Rice Cake with Peanut Butter

Spicy Beefsteak Kebabs

Snack: Celery Sticks with Goat Cheese and Green Olives

Mexican Style Protein Bowl

Week 4

Day 1:

Breakfast 'Pizza'

Snack: Greek Yogurt with Strawberries

Pancetta-wrapped Pollock with Potatoes

Snack: Cup of Popcorn

Vegan Friendly Dinner

Day 2:

Mexican Mocha Breakfast

Snack: Cherry Tomatoes with Cottage Cheese

Mediterranean Rice

Snack: Apple and Peanut Butter

Grilled Mushroom and Zucchini Burger

Day 3:

Fruit and Peanut Butter Smoothie

Snack: Avocado on Toast

Shrimp and Zucchini Linguine Pasta Salad

Snack: Blueberry Yogurt

Sweet and Sour Chicken

Day 4:

Pumpkin Pie Protein Pancakes

Snack: Yogurt with Dried Goji Berries

Spiced Chicken

Snack: Roasted Chickpeas

Dijon Mustard Halibut

Day 5:

Smoked Salmon and Avocado with Toast

Snack: Ham and Celery Sticks

Beef Meatball Pasta with Spinach

Snack: Nut Mix

Tofu Burger

Day 6:

High-protein Oatmeal

Snack: Bell Peppers with Cottage Cheese

Mexican Bean Chili

Snack: Yogurt with Tropical Fruit

Sushi Bowl

Day 7:

Protein-packed Scramble

Snack: Rice Cake with Peanut Butter

Trout with Potato Salad

Snack: Greek Yogurt with Strawberries

Tray Bake Chicken

2 extra days for a full month:

Day 1:

Whey Protein Muffins

Snack: Celery Sticks with Goat Cheese and Green Olives

Turkey Meatloaf with Whole Wheat Couscous

Snack: Apple and Peanut Butter

Tuna Melt

Day 2:

Tuna Stuffed Bell Peppers

Snack: Blueberry Yogurt

Stuffed Eggs with Pita Bread

Snack: Nut Mix

Chicken with Pineapple and Bell Peppers

BODYBUILDING MEAL RECIPES

BREAKFAST

1. Early Riser Breakfast

Snap your body out of a catabolic state and into a muscle-building one with this high-protein, high-carb oven-cooked breakfast. The grapefruit and asparagus make sure you get more than half a day's worth of vitamin C.

Ingredients (1serving):

6 egg whites

½ cup cooked quinoa and brown rice mix

3 asparagus spears, sliced

½ pink grapefruit

1 small red bell pepper, sliced

1 scoop flavorless whey protein powder

1 clove garlic, crushed

olive oil spray

pepper, salt

Prep time: 10 min

Cooking time: 15-20 min

Preparation:

Heat the oven to 200C fan/ gas 6. Lightly spray a cast iron skillet with olive oil.

In a medium bowl, whisk the egg whites with a pinch of salt and pepper until frothy.

Add the cooked brown rice and quinoa to the skillet; pour in the egg whites then the asparagus pieces and the bell pepper slices.

Bake in the oven for 15-20 min or until the eggs are cooked.

Nutritional value per serving: 407kcal, 52g protein, 40g carbs (5g fiber, 8g sugar), 2g fat, 15% calcium, 12% iron, 19% magnesium, 26% vitamin A, 63% vitamin C, 48% vitamin K, 12% vitamin B1, 69% vitamin B2, 26% vitamin B9.

2. Power Bowl

A breakfast with an appropriate name, the power bowl combines high in protein egg whites with energy fueling oatmeal. The walnuts add healthy fats and the honey tops everything with a bit of sweetness.

Ingredients (1 serving):

6 egg whites

½ cup instant oatmeal, cooked

1/8 cup walnuts

¼ cup berries

1 teaspoon raw honey

Cinnamon

Prep time: 10 min

Cooking time: 5 min

Preparation:

Whisk the egg whites until frothy then cook them in a skillet on low heat.

Combine the oatmeal and the egg whites in a bowl; add the cinnamon and raw honey and mix.

Top with berries, banana and walnuts.

Nutritional value per serving: 344kcal, 30g protein, 33g carbs (3g fiber, 23g sugar), 11g fat (2 saturated), 10% iron, 15% magnesium, 10% vitamin B1, 11% vitamin B2, 15% vitamin B5.

3. Tuna Stuffed Bell Peppers

This is a quick and nutritious recipe that provides a massive amount of B12. High in protein, tuna is an excellent breakfast option for muscle building and if you want to add some carbs to your meal, a piece of whole wheat toast is a great choice.

Ingredients (2 servings):

2 cans of tuna in water (185g), half drained

3 hard-boiled eggs

1 spring onion, finely chopped

5 small pickles, diced

salt, pepper

4 bell peppers, halved, with the seeds cleaned

Prep time: 5 min

Cooking time: 10 min

Preparation:

Combine the tuna, eggs, spring onion, pickles and seasoning in a food processor and mix until smooth.

Fill the halves of the bell peppers with the composition and serve.

Nutritional value per serving: 480kcal, 46g protein, 16g fat (4g saturated), 8g carbs (2g fiber, 4g sugar), 28%

magnesium, 94% vitamin A, 400% vitamin C, 12% vitamin E, 67% vitamin K, 18% vitamin B1, 32% vitamin B2, 90% vitamin B3, 20% vitamin B5, 56% vitamin B6, 18% vitamin B9, 284% vitamin B12.

4. Greek Yogurt with Flaxseeds and Apple

Branch out from the traditional egg white muscle-building breakfast and try some high-protein Greek Yogurt flavored with apple. Use whole flaxseeds to maximize your fiber intake and keep them in water overnight to get them soft and easily digestible.

Ingredients (1 serving):

1 cup Greek yogurt

1 apple, thinly sliced

2 tablespoons flaxseeds

¼ teaspoon cinnamon

1 teaspoon Stevia

A sprinkle of salt

Prep time: 5 min

Cooking time: 45 min

Preparation:

Preheat the oven to 190C fan/ gas 5. Place the apple slices in a non-stick pan, sprinkle them with cinnamon, Stevia and a dash of salt, cover them and bake for 45 min/ until tender. Remove them from the oven and allow them to cool for 30 min.

Place the Greek yogurt in a bowl then top with apples and flaxseeds and serve.

Nutritional value per serving: 422kcal, 22g protein, 39g carbs (7g fiber, 22 g sugar), 21g fat (8 g saturated), 14% calcium, 22% magnesium, 14% vitamin C, 24% vitamin B1, 13% vitamin B12.

5.   Bell Pepper Rings with 'Fit Grits'

A tasty and special looking meal, the bell pepper rings with 'Fit Grits' fuel your muscles and give you enough energy to power through your day. Full of color and nutrients, this breakfast is high in vitamin B1.

Ingredients (1 serving):

6 egg whites

2 eggs

¼ cup brown rice farina

1 cup raw spinach

½ green bell pepper

1 cup of cherry tomatoes

olive oil spray

salt, pepper

Prep time: 10 min

Cooking time: 15 min

Preparation:

Whisk the egg whites with a pinch of salt and pepper until frothy. Heat some oil in a non-stick frying pan and cook the egg whites and farina. Add the spinach, mix together and cook until the spinach has wilted.

Lightly spray a skillet with olive oil and set on medium heat. Cut the bell peppers horizontally to create 2 rings, place them in the skillet and crack the eggs inside the bell peppers. Let them cook until the eggs turn white.

Place the egg-farina mixture and cooked pepper rings on a plate and serve with cherry tomatoes.

Nutritional value per serving : 495kcal, 45g protein, 45g carbs (3g fiber, 7g sugar), 11g fat (3g saturated), 9% calcium, 14% iron, 20% magnesium, 35% vitamin A, 32% vitamin C, 91% vitamin B2, 22% vitamin B5, 12% vitamin B6, 15% vitamin B12.

6. Almond Milk Smoothie

10 minutes is all you need to fix this high in vitamin D and B1 almond milk smoothie. You can fix a big batch and keep it in the freezer making this smoothie a perfect option for a quick breakfast to go.

Ingredients (2 serving):

1 cup almond milk

1 cup frozen mixed berries

1 cup spinach

1 scoop banana flavored protein powder

1 tablespoon chia seeds

Prep time: 10 min

No cooking

Preparation:

Mix all the ingredients in a blender until smooth, pour into 2 glasses and serve.

Nutritional value per serving: 295kcal, 26g protein, 32g carbs (4g fiber, 13g sugar), 9g fat, 40% calcium, 20% iron, 12% magnesium, 50% vitamin A, 40% vitamin C, 25% vitamin D, 57% vitamin E, 213% vitamin B1, 18% vitamin B9.

7. Pumpkin Pie Protein Pancakes

Forget about flour and try oat pancakes with a delicious addition of fresh pumpkin. Topple some calorie-free syrup and enjoy a high-protein breakfast that tastes as good as a cheat meal.

Ingredients (1 serving):

1/3 cup old-fashioned oats

¼ cup pumpkin

½ cup egg whites

1 scoop cinnamon protein powder

½ teaspoon cinnamon

olive oil spray

Prep time: 5 min

Cooking time: 5 min

Preparation:

Mix all the ingredients together in a bowl. Spray a medium-sized skillet with olive oil then place on medium heat.

Pour in the batter, and once you see tiny bubbles appear on the top of the pancake, flip. When each side is golden, remove the pancake and serve.

Nutritional value per serving: 335kcal, 39g protein, 37g carbs (6g fiber, 1 g sugar), 6g fat, 14% calcium, 15% iron, 26% magnesium, 60% vitamin A, 26% vitamin B1, 37% vitamin B2, 10% vitamin B5, 31% vitamin B6.

8. High-protein Oatmeal

Lasso in a hearty helping of carbs that will keep you satiated for hours, while the protein powder and almonds will deliver a protein-packed start to your day. If you prefer you oatmeal with a fruity taste, use banana flavored protein powder.

Ingredients (1 serving):

2 packets of instant oatmeal (28g packet)

¼ cup ground almonds

1 scoop of vanilla flavored whey protein powder

1 tablespoon cinnamon

Prep time: 5 min

Cooking time: 5 min

Preparation:

Pour the instant oatmeal into a bowl, mix with the protein powder and cinnamon. Add hot water and mix. Top with crushed almonds and serve.

Nutritional value per serving: 436kcal, 33g protein, 45g carbs (10g fiber, 4g sugar), 15g fat (1g saturated), 17% calcium, 19% iron, 37% magnesium, 44% vitamin E, 21% vitamin B1, 21% vitamin B2.

9. Protein-packed Scramble

Feed your muscles and push through an intense workout with this 51g protein meal. These scrambled egg whites with vegetables and turkey sausage have the added value of being packed with carbs and overall high amounts of vitamins.

Ingredients (1 serving):

8 egg whites

2 link turkey sausages, chopped

1 large onion, diced

1 cup red bell peppers, diced

2 tomatoes, diced

2 cups raw spinach, chopped

1 teaspoon olive oil

salt and pepper

Prep time: 10 min

Cooking time: 10-15 min

Preparation:

Whisk the egg whites with a pinch of salt and pepper until frothy, then set aside.

Heat the oil in a large non-stick pan, drizzle the onions and peppers and sauté until they are tender. Season with salt and pepper. Add the turkey sausage and cook until it is golden brown then lower the heat and add the egg whites and scramble.

When the eggs are almost done, add the tomato and spinach, cook for 2 min and serve.

Nutritional value per serving: 475kcal, 51g protein, 37g carbs (10g fiber, 18g sugar), 10g fat (2g saturated), 14% calcium, 23% iron, 37% magnesium, 255% vitamin A, 516% vitamin C, 25% vitamin E, 397% vitamin K, 22% vitamin B1, 112% vitamin B2, 29% vitamin B3, 19% vitamin B5, 51% vitamin B6, 65% vitamin B9.

10.   Fruit and Peanut Butter Smoothie

What better way to get your day's worth of calcium than with this strawberry flavored smoothie? High in minerals, vitamins, protein and energy fueling carbs, this smoothie is a perfect way to kick-start your day.

Ingredients (1 serving):

15 medium-sized strawberries

1 1/3 tablespoons peanut butter

85g tofu

½ cup fat free yogurt

¾ cup skim milk

1 scoop protein powder

8 ice cubes

Prep time: 5min

No cooking

Preparation:

Pour the milk into the blender then the yogurt and the rest of the ingredients. Blend until mixture is completely blended and frothy. Pour into a glass and serve.

Nutritional value per serving: 472kcal, 45g protein, 40g carbs (6g fiber, 31g sugar), 13g fat (4g saturated), 110% calcium, 35% iron, 27% magnesium, 30% vitamin A, 190% vitamin C, 11% vitamin E, 13% vitamin B1, 24% vitamin B2, 10% vitamin B5, 18% vitamin B6, 17% vitamin B9, 12% vitamin B12.

11. Whey Protein Muffins

With a healthy dose of oats and a serving of chocolate whey protein powder, these muffins are a great breakfast alternative to regular oats. Paired with a glass of milk, this meal makes sure that you get a good amount of calcium and vitamin D to go with the nice protein and carbs serving.

Ingredients (4 muffins-2 servings):

1 cup rolled oats

1 large whole egg

5 large egg whites

½ scoop chocolate whey protein powder

olive oil spray

2 cups of low fat milk, to serve

Prep time: 2 min

Cooking time: 15 min

Preparation:

Preheat the oven to 190C fan/ gas 5.

Blend all the ingredients together for 30s. Spray the muffin tin with olive oil then batter up into four muffins. Place in the oven for 15 min.

Remove from the oven, let them cool and serve with the glass of milk.

Nutritional value per serving (includes milk): 330kcal, 28g protein, 37g carbs (9g fiber, 13g sugar), 6g fat (5g saturated), 37% calcium, 22% iron, 19% magnesium, 12% vitamin A, 34% vitamin D, 44% vitamin B1, 66% vitamin B2, 25% vitamin B5, 11% vitamin B6, 24% vitamin B12.

12. Smoked Salmon and Avocado with Toast

Are you in for a tough workout and low on time? It only takes 5 min to piece together this savory breakfast. Both the salmon and avocado are high in healthy acids and this meal has enough protein and carbs to keep you motivated.

Ingredients (2 servings):

300g smoked salmon

2 medium-sized ripe avocados, stoned and peeled

Juice from ½ lemon

handful tarragon leaves, chopped

2 slices of whole wheat bread, toasted

Prep time: 5 min

No cooking time

Preparation:

Cut the avocados into chunks and toss in the lemon juice. Twist and fold the smoked salmon pieces, place them on serving plates, then scatter with the avocado and tarragon. Serve with whole wheat toast.

Nutritional value per serving: 550kcal, 34g protein, 37g carbs (12g fiber, 4g sugar), 30g fat (5g saturated), 17% iron, 24% magnesium, 25% vitamin C, 27% vitamin E, 42% vitamin K, 16% vitamin B1, 24% vitamin B2, 55% vitamin B3, 35% vitamin B5, 40% vitamin B6, 35% vitamin B9, 81% vitamin B12.

13. Breakfast 'Pizza'

Forget about the high-calorie, non-nutritious slice of pizza and replace it with this delicious substitute. Healthy and filling, it only takes 20 min to make and it's not only high in protein, but also in minerals and vitamins.

Ingredients (1 serving):

1 small whole wheat pita

3 egg whites

1 egg

¼ cup low-fat mozzarella cheese

1 spring onion, sliced

¼ cup mushrooms, diced

¼ cup bell peppers, diced

2 slices turkey bacon, chopped

1 teaspoon olive oil

salt and pepper

Prep time: 10 min

Cooking time: 10 min

Preparation:

Whisk the eggs with a pinch of salt and pepper and add the diced vegetables.

Bend the edges of the pita bread to create a bowl. Brush both sides with the olive oil and place the pita bread on the grill, dome side down. Cook until golden then flip it on the other side.

Pour the egg mix into the pita and cook until the eggs are nearly done, add the turkey bacon, spring onion and cheese. Cook until the cheese had melted and serve.

Nutritional value per serving: 350kcal, 33g protein, 12g carbs (3g fiber, 4g sugar), 15g fat (6 saturated), 32% calcium, 19% iron, 15% magnesium, 36% vitamin A, 88% vitamin C, 72% vitamin K, 21% vitamin B1, 71% vitamin B2, 22% vitamin B3, 14% vitamin B5, 21% vitamin B6, 25% vitamin B9, 29% vitamin B12.

14. Mexican Mocha Breakfast

Top your favorite cup of oats with a healthy serving of almond milk and enjoy a quickly-made high-fiber breakfast. The cayenne pepper is perfect for adding a little oomph to your oatmeal.

Ingredients (1 serving):

½ cup rolled oats

1 scoop chocolate protein powder

½ tablespoon cinnamon

½ teaspoon cayenne pepper

1 cup unsweetened almond milk

1 tablespoon unsweetened cocoa powder

Prep time: 5 min

Cooking time: 3 min

Preparation:

Mix all the ingredients in a microwave-safe bowl. Heat in the microwave for 2 ½ -3 min then serve.

Nutritional value per serving: 304kcal, 27g protein, 38g carbs (8g fiber, 3g sugar), 7g fat, 32% calcium, 15% iron, 25% magnesium, 10% vitamin A, 25% vitamin D, 51% vitamin E, 12% vitamin B1.

15. Blueberry Lemon Pancakes

A warm, filling breakfast, this blueberry pancake enriched by the lemony flavor is a simple and tasty way of getting that high-powered meal that you need to start your day. Spread a tablespoon of Greek yogurt on top of your pancake if you like.

Ingredients (1 serving):

1/3 cup oat bran

5 egg whites

½ cup blueberries

1 scoop flavorless whey protein powder

½ teaspoon baking soda

1 teaspoon grated lemon peel

1 tablespoon lemon drink mix

olive oil spray

Prep time: 5 min

Cooking time: 5 min

Preparation:

Combine all the ingredients in a large bowl, mix and whisk until smooth.

Cook the batch in a sprayed skilled on medium-high temperature until bubbles form on the surface. Flip over and cook until each side is dark golden brown. Remove the pancake and serve.

Nutritional value per serving: 340kcal, 47g protein, 37g carbs (6g fiber, 14g sugar), 5g fat, 10% iron, 25% magnesium, 12% vitamin C, 19% vitamin K, 26% vitamin B1, 58% vitamin B2.

LUNCH

16. Mediterranean Rice

Turn the tired can of tuna into a delicious dish that is a perfect starter for an afternoon of exercise. The high amount of carbs will fuel a thorough workout and the protein will make sure that your muscles recuperate from the effort.

Ingredients (1 serving):

1 can of tuna in oil, drained

100g brown rice

¼ avocado, chopped

¼ red onion, sliced

juice from ½ lemon

salt and pepper

Prep time: 5 min

Cooking time: 20 min

Preparation:

Boil the brown rice for approximately 20 min then place in a bowl with the onion, tuna and avocado. Add the lemon juice and mix all the ingredients. Season with salt and pepper to taste and serve.

Nutritional value per serving: 590kcal, 32g protein, 80g carbs (7g fiber, 1g sugar), 14g fat (5g saturated), 22% iron, 52% magnesium, 101% vitamin D, 18% vitamin E, 107% vitamin K, 32% vitamin B1, 134% vitamin B3, 26% vitamin B5, 39% vitamin B6, 15% vitamin B9, 63% vitamin B12.

17. Spiced Chicken

Chicken is perfect for a high protein muscle building meal. High in nutrients across the board, this simple, tasty meal can be paired with a serving of your choice of carbs.

Ingredients (2 servings):

3 boneless chicken breasts cut in half

175g low-fat yogurt

5cm piece cucumber, finely chopped

2 tablespoons Thai red curry paste

2 tablespoons cilantro, chopped

2 cups raw spinach, to serve.

Prep time: 5 min

Cooking time: 35-40 min

Preparation:

Preheat the oven to 190C fan/ gas 5. Put the chicken in a dish in one layer. Blend a third of the yogurt, the curry paste and two thirds of the cilantro, add salt and pour over the chicken, making sure the meat is evenly coated. Leave for 30 min (or in the fridge overnight).

Lift the chicken onto a rack in a roasting tin for 35-40 min, until golden.

Heat water in a pan and wilt the spinach.

Mix the rest of the yogurt and cilantro, add the cucumber and stir. Pour the mix over the chicken and serve with the cooked spinach.

Nutritional value per serving: 275kcal, 43g protein, 8g carbs (1g fiber, 8g sugar), 3g fat (1g saturated), 20% calcium, 15% iron, 25% magnesium, 56% vitamin A, 18% vitamin C, 181% vitamin K, 16% vitamin B1, 26% vitamin B2, 133% vitamin B3, 25% vitamin B5, 67% vitamin B6, 19% vitamin B9, 22% vitamin B12.

18. Stuffed Eggs with Pita Bread

Get your fill of omega-3 fatty acids with this rich salmon dish. High in vitamins and minerals, this filling meal is a great way of boosting yourself with energy and powering through your day.

Ingredients (2 servings):

1 canned salmon in water (450g)

2 eggs

1 large spring onions, finely chopped

2 large leafs of lettuce

10 cherry tomatoes

1 tablespoon Greek yogurt

a large whole wheat pita bread, cut in half

sea salt and pepper

Prep time: 10 min

Cooking time: 10 min

Preparation:

Boil the eggs, peel them and slice them in half then remove the yolks and place them in a bowl.

Add the canned salmon, 1 tablespoon of yogurt, the spring onion and the seasonings to the bowl. Mix all the ingredients together and stuff the egg whites. Serve with pita bread stuffed with lettuce and tomatoes.

Nutritional value per serving: 455kcal, 45g protein, 24g carbs (3g fiber, 2g sugar), 36g fat (10g saturated), 59% calcium, 22% iron, 21% magnesium, 30% vitamin A, 24% vitamin C, 43% vitamin K, 11% vitamin B1, 36% vitamin B2, 60% vitamin B3, 20% vitamin B5, 41% vitamin B6, 20% vitamin B9, 20% vitamin B12.

19. Chicken Caesar Wraps

These chicken wraps make a great portable meal that will make sure that you keep your protein levels high throughout the day. Throw in some baby spinach and make a more green friendly meal.

Ingredients (1 serving):

85g chicken breast, baked

2 whole wheat tortillas

1 cup lettuce

50g non-fat yogurt

1 teaspoon anchovy paste

1 teaspoon dry mustard powder

1 clove garlic, cooked

½ medium cucumber, chopped

Prep time: 5 min

No cooking

Preparation:

Combine the anchovy paste, garlic and yogurt then toss and coat the lettuce and cucumbers. Split the mix in 2, add to the tortillas and then place half the chicken in each tortilla. Wrap up and serve.

Nutritional value per serving (2 tortillas): 460kcal, 41g protein, 57g carbs (7g fiber, 9g sugar), 10g fat (2g saturated), 11% calcium, 22% vitamin K, 13% vitamin B2, 59% vitamin B3, 12% vitamin B5, 29% vitamin B6, 10% vitamin B12.

20. Baked Salmon with Grilled Asparagus

A classic dish, made more interesting by a marinade of lemon juice and mustard, this grilled salmon goes well with the garlicky asparagus spears. Treat yourself to a great combination of protein and vitamins.

Ingredients (1 serving):

140g wild salmon

1 ½ cup asparagus

Marinade:

1 tablespoon garlic, minced

1 tablespoon Dijon mustard

lemon juice from ½ lemon

1 teaspoon olive oil

Prep time: 5 min

Cooking time: 15 min

Preparation:

Preheat oven to 200C fan/ gas 6.

In a bowl, mix the lemon juice, half the garlic, olive oil and mustard, pour the marinade over the salmon and make sure it is completely covered. Place the marinating salmon in the fridge for at least one hour.

Cut the bottom stems off the asparagus spears. Set a nonstick skillet on medium/high heat, toss the asparagus with the remaining garlic and sear for about 5 min, rolling the asparagus on all sides.

Place the salmon on a baking sheet and bake for 10 min then serve with the grilled asparagus.

Nutritional value: 350kcal, 43g protein, 7g carbs (5g fiber, 1 g sugar), 16g fat (1 saturated), 17% iron, 20% magnesium, 48% vitamin A, 119% vitamin C, 17% vitamin E, 288% vitamin K, 39% vitamin B1, 60% vitamin B2, 90% vitamin B3, 33% vitamin B5, 74% vitamin B6, 109% vitamin B9, 75% vitamin B12.

21. Beef Meatball Pasta with Spinach

A high-protein pasta meal that makes the most of the beef and spinach pairing. Not only is it all-round vitamin packed, but it also contains a hearty amount of magnesium which helps regulate muscle contraction.

Ingredients (2 servings):

For meatballs:

170g lean ground beef

½ cup raw spinach, shredded

1 tablespoon minced garlic

¼ cup red onion, diced

1 teaspoon cumin

sea salt and pepper

For Pasta:

100g wheat spinach pasta

10 cherry tomatoes

2 cups raw spinach

¼ cup marinara

2 tablespoons low-fat parmesan cheese

Prep time: 15 min

Cooking time: 30 min

Preparation:

Preheat oven to 200C/ gas 6.

Mix together the ground beef, raw spinach, garlic, red onion and salt and pepper to taste. Mix thoroughly with your hands until the spinach is completely mixed into the meat.

Form two or three meatballs, roughly the same size then place them on a baking sheet in the oven for 10-12 minutes.

Cook the pasta according to the instructions on the pack. Drain the pasta and stir in the tomatoes, spinach and cheese. Add the meatballs and serve.

Nutritional value per serving: 470kcal, 33g protein, 50g carbs (6g fiber, 5g sugar), 12g fat (5g saturated), 17% calcium, 28% iron, 74% magnesium, 104% vitamin A, 38% vitamin C, 11% vitamin E, 361% vitamin K, 16% vitamin B1,

20% vitamin B2, 45% vitamin B3, 11% vitamin B5, 45% vitamin B6, 35% vitamin B9, 37% vitamin B12.

22. Stuffed Chicken Breast with Brown Rice

Brown rice is an excellent way of introducing quality carbs to your diet. Couple it with high-protein chicken breast and some vegetables and you have a delicious power lunch.

Ingredients (1 serving):

170g chicken breast

½ cup raw spinach

50g brown rice

1 spring onion, diced

1 tomato, sliced

1 tablespoon feta cheese

Prep time: 10 min

Cooking time: 30 min

Preparation:

Preheat the oven to 190C fan/ gas 5.

Slice the chicken breast down the middle to make it look like a butterfly. Season the chicken with salt and pepper, then open it and layer spinach, feta cheese and tomato slices on one side. Fold the chicken breast and use a toothpick to hold it closed then bake for 20 min.

Boil the brown rice then add the garlic and chopped onion. Fill a plate with brown rice, place the chicken on top and serve.

Nutritional value per serving: 469kcal, 48g protein, 46g carbs (5g fiber, 6g sugar), 8g fat (5g saturated), 22% calcium, 18% iron, 38% magnesium, 55% vitamin A, 43% vitamin C, 169% vitamin K, 28% vitamin B1, 28% vitamin B2, 103% vitamin B3, 28% vitamin B5, 70% vitamin B6, 23% vitamin B9, 17% vitamin B12.

23. Shrimp and Zucchini Linguine Pasta Salad

A cheat pasta meal with a serving of shredded zucchini and steamed shrimp flavored with all manners of sesame. This combination of ingredients makes for a light lunch with a high-protein content.

Ingredients (1 serving):

170g steamed shrimp

1 large zucchini, chopped

¼ cup red onion, sliced

1 cup bell peppers, sliced

1 tablespoon roasted Tahini butter

1 teaspoon sesame oil

1 teaspoon sesame seeds

Prep time: 10 min

No cooking

Preparation:

Cut the zucchini using a shredder in order to make raw linguine.

In a bowl, mix tahini and sesame oil.

Place all the ingredients in a large bowl, pour the Tahini sauce and toss it to make sure all sides are covered in sauce. Sprinkle some sesame seeds and serve.

Nutritional value per serving: 420kcal, 45g protein, 26g carbs (10g fiber, 12g sugar), 18g fat (2g saturated), 19% calcium, 47% iron, 48% magnesium, 33% vitamin A, 303% vitamin C, 17% vitamin E, 31% vitamin K, 38% vitamin B1, 36% vitamin B2, 38% vitamin B3, 13% vitamin B5, 66% vitamin B6, 35% vitamin B9, 42% vitamin B12.

24. Turkey Meatloaf with Whole Wheat Couscous

Cooked in a muffin pan, this turkey meatloaf makes sure that you minimize you saturated fats intake. Mix it up a little by adding bell pepper or mushrooms instead of onion into the meatballs and by seasoning with a pinch of ground garlic.

Ingredients (1 serving):

140g lean ground turkey

¾ cup red onions, diced

1 cup raw spinach

1/3 cup low sodium marinara sauce

½ cup whole wheat couscous, boiled

choice of seasoning: Parsley, Basil, Coriander

pepper, salt

olive oil spray

Prep time: 5 min

Cooking time: 20 min

Preparation:

Preheat oven to 200C fan/ gas 6.

Season turkey with your choice of seasoning and add the diced onions.

Light spray your muffin pan with olive oil, place the ground turkey inside the muffin holders. Top each turkey meatball with 1 tablespoon marinara sauce, then place in the oven and bake for 8-10 min.

Serve with couscous.

Nutritional value per serving: 460kcal, 34g protein, 53g carbs (4g fiber, 7g sugar), 12g fat (4g saturated), 12% calcium, 15% iron, 10% magnesium, 16% vitamin A, 15% vitamin C, 11% vitamin E, 16% vitamin K, 11% vitamin B1, 25% vitamin B3, 16% vitamin B6, 11% vitamin B9.

25. Tuna Burger and Salad

The tuna burger is high in protein and carbs, making it an excellent choice for a workout day meal. Fix it differently every time and keep it interesting by switching between vegetables and seasoning your salad dressing.

Ingredients (1 serving):

1 canned chunk tuna (165g)

1 egg white

½ cup chopped mushrooms

2 cups lettuce, shredded

¼ cup dried oats

1 teaspoon olive oil

1 tablespoons low-fat salad dressing (of preference)

small bunch of oregano, chopped

1 whole wheat medium roll cut in half

Prep time: 10 min

Cooking time: 10 min

Preparation:

Mix together the egg white, tuna, dry oats, oregano and form a patty.

Heat the oil in a non-stick pan on medium heat, place the patty on and flip it to make sure it cooks on both sides.

Cut the whole wheat roll in half, horizontally, place the patty between the 2 pieces.

Mix the vegetables in a bowl, add the salad dressing and serve next to the tuna burger.

Nutritional value per serving: 560kcal, 52g protein, 76g carbs (13g fiber, 7g sugar), 10g fat (1g saturated), 11% calcium, 35% iron, 38% magnesium, 16% vitamin A, 16% vitamin K, 35% vitamin B1, 33% vitamin B2, 24% vitamin B3, 28% vitamin B5, 41% vitamin B6, 21% vitamin B9, 82% vitamin B12.

26. Spicy Beefsteak Kebabs

This spicy kebab is served with a side of baked potato, making it not only a muscle building meal but also a great way of introducing eyesight protecting vitamin A to your diet. Add a tablespoon of low-fat yogurt to your potato to make it more refreshing.

Ingredients (1 serving):

140g lean beef flank steak

200g sweet potato

1 bell pepper, chopped

½ medium zucchini, chopped

minced garlic

pepper, salt

Prep time: 15 min

Cooking time: 55 min

Preparation:

Preheat oven to 200C fan/ gas 6. Wrap the sweet potato in a foil, place in the oven and bake for 45 min.

Cut the flank steak into small pieces, season with salt, pepper and garlic. Assemble the kebab, alternating between beef, zucchini and bell pepper.

Place the kebab on a baking sheet and bake for 10 min. Serve with the sweet potato.

Nutritional value per serving: 375kcal, 38g protein, 49g carbs (9g fiber, 12g sugar), 4g fat (1g saturated), 24% iron, 27% magnesium, 581% vitamin A, 195% vitamin C, 21% vitamin K, 22% vitamin B1, 28% vitamin B2, 61% vitamin B3, 28% vitamin B5, 92% vitamin B6, 20% vitamin B9, 30% vitamin B12.

27. Trout with Potatoes Salad

Want to make sure that you are not lacking in vitamin B12? Try this hearty portion of trout, paired with a nutrient and vitamin packed fresh-tasting potato salad.

Ingredients (2 servings):

2*140g trout fillets

250g waxy potatoes, halved

4 teaspoons yogurt

4 teaspoons reduced-fat mayonnaise

1 tablespoon capers, rinsed

4 small cornichons, sliced

2 spring onions, finely sliced

¼ cucumber, diced

1 lemon, zest from ½

Prep time: 10 min

Cooking time: 20 min

Preparation:

Boil the potatoes in salted water for 15 min until they are just tender. Drain and rinse under cold water, then drain again.

Heat the grill.

Mix the mayonnaise and yogurt and season with some lemon juice. Stir the mix into the potatoes with the capers, most of the spring onion, cucumber and cornichons. Scatter the salad with the rest of the onions.

Season the trout, grill on a baking sheet, skin-side down, until just cooked. Scatter with the lemon zest and serve with the potato salad.

Nutritional value per serving: 420kcal, 38g protein, 28g carbs (3g fiber, 6g sugar), 13g fat (3g saturated), 12% calcium, 11% iron, 22% magnesium, 29% vitamin C, 59% vitamin K, 21% vitamin B1, 18% vitamin B2, 12% vitamin B3, 22% vitamin B5, 43% vitamin B6, 18% vitamin B9, 153% vitamin B12.

28. Mexican Bean Chili

A high in protein midday meal, this dish is a great way of getting 1/3 of your daily required amount of fiber. Though it has enough nutrients to be a stand-alone meal, it can also be served on top of a bed of brown rice.

Ingredients (2 servings):

250g minced beef

200g caned baked beans

75ml beef stock

½ onion, diced

½ red pepper, diced

1 teaspoon chipotle paste

1 teaspoon olive oil

½ teaspoon chili powder

1 cup brown rice, boiled (optional)

coriander leaves, o serve

Prep time: 5 min

Cooking time: 45 min

Preparation:

Heat the oil in a non-stick pan over medium heat then fry the onion and red pepper until softened. Increase the heat, add the chili powder and cook for 2 min before adding the minced beef. Cook until browned and all the liquid has evaporated.

Tip in the beef stock, baked beans and chipotle paste. Simmer over a low heat for 20 min, then season and scatter with coriander leaves and serve with the boiled rice.

Nutritional value per serving (without rice): 402kcal, 34g protein, 19g carbs (5g fiber, 10g sugar), 14g fat (5g saturated), 29% iron, 15% magnesium, 42% vitamin C, 11% vitamin B1, 16% vitamin B2, 34% vitamin B3, 40% vitamin B6, 18% vitamin B9, 52% vitamin B12.

½ cup of rice: 108kcal

29. Beef and Broccoli Noodles

A convenient, tasty dish, the beef and broccoli noodles take only 20 min to prepare, making it a great choice for a busy day. You can serve with a few slices of red chili for some extra spice.

Ingredients (2 servings):

2 cups egg noodles

200g beef stir-fry strips

1 spring onion, sliced

½ head broccoli, small florets

1 teaspoon sesame oil

For the sauce:

1 ½ tablespoons low-salt soy sauce

1 teaspoon tomato ketchup

1 garlic clove, crushed

1 tablespoon oyster sauce

¼ knob ginger, finely grated

1 teaspoon white wine vinegar

Prep time: 10 min

Cooking time: 10 min

Preparation:

Mix the ingredients for the sauce. Boil the noodles according to the pack instructions. Tip in the broccoli when they are almost ready. Leave for a few minutes then drain the noodles and broccoli.

Heat the oil in a wok until very hot then stir-fry the beef for 2-3 minutes until browned. Tip the sauce, stir, and let it simmer for a few moments then turn off the heat.

Stir the beef into the noodles, scatter with the spring onion and serve immediately.

Nutritional value per serving: 352kcal, 33g protein, 39g carbs (5g fiber, 5g sugar), 9g fat (2g saturated), 20% iron, 20% magnesium, 20% vitamin A, 224% vitamin C, 214% vitamin K, 14% vitamin B1, 19% vitamin B2, 43% vitamin B3, 18% vitamin B5, 50% vitamin B6, 31% vitamin B9, 23% vitamin B12.

30. Pancetta-wrapped Pollock with Potatoes

This light and fresh-tasting dish provides a lot of energy and is high in protein, making it an ideal option for a midday meal. The pollock can be substituted for another sustainable white fish, while the olives can be replaced by sundried tomatoes.

Ingredients (2 servings):

2* 140g pollock fillets

4 slices pancetta

300g new potatoes

100g green beans

30g kalamata olives

juice and zest from 1 lemon

2 tablespoons olive oil

a few tarragon sprigs, leaves picked

Prep time: 10 min

Cooking time 15 min

Preparation:

Heat oven to 200C fan/ gas 6. Boil the potatoes for 10-12 min until tender, add the beans for the final 2-3 min. Drain well, slice the potatoes in half and tip into a baking dish. Toss with the olives, lemon zest and oil and season well.

Season the fish and wrap with the pancetta then place it on top of the potatoes. Bake for 10-12 min until cooked through, then add the lemon juice, scatter with tarragon and serve.

Nutritional value per serving: 525kcal, 46g protein, 36g carbs (5g fiber, 3g sugar), 31g fat (8g saturated), 10% iron, 31% magnesium, 63% vitamin C, 18% vitamin K, 15% vitamin B1, 13% vitamin B2, 14% vitamin B3, 25% vitamin B6, 73% vitamin B12.

DINNER

31. Sushi Bowl

This is a low-calorie sushi bowl that substitutes rice for cauliflower flavored with garlic, soy sauce and lime juice for extra taste. Use the seaweed sheets to wrap the veggies and salmon and make a mini roll.

Ingredients (2 servings):

170g smoked salmon

1 medium-sized avocado

½ head cauliflower, steamed and chopped

1/3 cup carrot, shredded

½ teaspoon cayenne

1.2 teaspoon garlic powder

1 tablespoon low-sodium soy sauce

2 seaweed sheets

Juice from ½ lime

Prep time: 10 min

No cooking

Preparation:

Place the cauliflower, carrots, soy sauce, garlic, lime juice and cayenne in a food processor. Stop blending before the mix turns into a paste. Serve next to the salmon and seaweed sheets.

Nutritional value per serving: 272kcal, 20g protein, 13g carbs (7g fiber, 4g sugar), 16g fat (1g saturated), 10% iron, 14% magnesium, 73% vitamin A, 88% vitamin C, 13% vitamin E, 40% vitamin K, 18% vitamin B1, 15% vitamin B2, 31% vitamin B3, 21% vitamin B5, 31% vitamin B6, 26% vitamin B9, 45% vitamin B12.

32. Sweet and Sour Chicken

The sweet and sour chicken is a simple, delicious recipe that has a place in every fit kitchen. It is high in protein and vitamins and goes well with steamed broccoli florets.

Ingredients (2 servings):

300g chicken breasts cut into bite-sized pieces

1 teaspoon garlic salt

¼ cup low sodium chicken broth

¼ cup white vinegar

¼ no-calorie sweetener

¼ teaspoon black pepper

1 teaspoon low-sodium soy sauce

3 teaspoons low-sugar ketchup

arrowroot

400g broccoli florets, steamed

Prep time: 10 min

Cooking time 15 min

Preparation:

Place the chicken in a large bowl and season with the garlic, pepper and salt, turning to coat. Cook the chicken over medium/high heat until done.

In the meantime, whisk together the chicken broth, sweetener, vinegar, ketchup and soy sauce in a sauce pan, bring the mix to a boil and turn to low heat. Add the arrowroot a little at a time and whisk briskly. Keep stirring for a few minutes.

Pour sauce over the cooked chicken and serve with a side of steamed broccoli.

Nutritional value per serving: 250kcal, 40g protein, 14g carbs (6g fiber, 4g sugar), 2g fat, 11% calcium, 14% iron, 20% magnesium, 24% vitamin A, 303% vitamin C, 254% vitamin K, 17% vitamin B1, 21% vitamin B2, 90% vitamin B3, 24% vitamin B5, 58% vitamin B6, 33% vitamin B9.

33. Garlicky Hummus

You only need 5 min to make this healthy, delicious meal. It is chock-full with magnesium and has a decent amount of protein considering the recipe is meatless. Grab a whole wheat tortilla and make this meal to go.

Ingredients (3 servings):

1*400g canned chickpeas (save 1/4 of the liquid)

¼ cup tahini

¼ cup lemon juice

1 clove garlic

1 tablespoon olive oil

¼ teaspoon ground ginger

¼ teaspoon ground cumin

2 spring onions, finely chopped

1 tomato, chopped

Prep time: 5 min

No cooking

Preparation:

Place the chickpeas, liquid, tahini, lemon juice, olive oil, garlic, cumin and ginger in a food processor and blend until smooth.

Stir in the tomato and scallions and season with salt and pepper. Serve next to slices of bell pepper.

Nutritional value per serving: 324kcal, 11g protein, 21g carbs (7g fiber, 1g sugar), 17g fat (2g saturated), 22% calcium, 54% iron, 135% magnesium, 10% vitamin A, 12% vitamin C, 33% vitamin K, 122% vitamin B1, 12% vitamin B2, 44% vitamin B3, 11% vitamin B5, 12% vitamin B6, 40% vitamin B9.

34. Chicken with Pineapple and Bell Peppers

Take a break from the usual chicken recipes and try this version with sweet, fresh pineapple. High in vitamin B3 and protein, this meal is also an important source of carbs. In tone with the change of pace, you can substitute the rice for quinoa.

Ingredients (1 serving):

140g boneless chicken breast,

1 tablespoon mustard

½ cup fresh pineapple, diced

½ cup bell peppers, diced

50g brown rice

Coconut oil spray

1 teaspoon cumin

salt and pepper

Prep time: 5 min

Cooking time: 15 min

Preparation:

Cut the chicken into small pieces then rub the mustard on the pieces and season with salt, pepper and cumin.

Set a skillet on medium heat and lightly spray with coconut oil, add the chicken and cook on all sides. When the chicken is almost finished, increase the heat and toss in the pineapple pieces and bell peppers, cook and make sure that all sides are brown. This should take 3-5 min.

Boil the brown rice and serve next to the chicken.

Nutritional value per serving: 377kcal, 37g protein, 50g carbs (6g fiber, 10g sugar), 1g fat, 12% iron, 33% magnesium, 168% vitamin C, 26% vitamin B1, 13% vitamin B2, 96% vitamin B3, 22% vitamin B5, 65% vitamin B6, 10% vitamin B9.

35. Mexican Style Protein Bowl

Give yourself a break from meat and throw these ingredients together for a tasty alternative to the usual. You can skip the fried fat and unhealthy calories and still get the flavor of a Mexican meal.

Ingredients:

1/3 cup cooked black beans

½ cup cooked brown rice

2 tablespoons salsa

¼ avocado, sliced

Prep time: 5 min

No cooking

Preparation:

Combine all the ingredients in a bowl and serve.

Nutritional value per serving: 307kcal, 11g protein, 48g carbs (11g fiber, 1g sugar), 7g fat (1g sugar), 26%

magnesium, 13% vitamin K, 16% vitamin B1, 11% vitamin B3, 17% vitamin B6, 30% vitamin B9.

36. Arugula Chicken Salad

The arugula leaves add satisfaction to this sweet and super healthy salad. Bountiful in vegetables and quality protein source, this meal can be enriched with a simple dressing of low-fat yogurt and garlic.

Ingredients (1 serving):

120g chicken breast

5 baby carrots, chopped

¼ red cabbage, chopped

½ cup arugula

1 tablespoon sunflower seeds

1 teaspoon olive oil

Prep time: 10 min

Cooking time: 10 min

Preparation:

Cut the chicken into bite-sized cubes. Heat the olive oil in a non-stick pan and fry the chicken until it is cooked. Set aside and allow cooling.

Place the carrots, arugula and cabbage in a large bowl. Top the salad with the cooled chicken and sunflower seeds and serve.

Nutritional value per serving: 311kcal, 30g protein, 9g carbs (1g fiber), 13g fat (1g saturated), 11% iron, 22% magnesium, 150% vitamin A, 25% vitamin C, 29% vitamin E, 32% vitamin K, 23% vitamin B1, 10% vitamin B2, 72% vitamin B3, 11% vitamin B5, 49% vitamin B6, 17% vitamin B9.

37. Dijon Mustard Halibut

This tangy halibut meal is a fast-and-easy way to get a hearty dose of protein. It's low in carbs and high in vitamins, making it a perfect choice for supper. The low calorie count allows you to double the sauce if you are feeling indulgent.

Ingredients (2 servings):

220g halibut

¼ onion, diced

1 red pepper, diced

1 clove garlic

1 tablespoon Dijon mustard

1 teaspoon Worcestershire sauce

1 teaspoon olive oil

juice from 1 lemon

a bunch of parsley

2 large carrots cut into sticks

1 cup broccoli florets

1 cup mushrooms, sliced

Prep time: 10 min

Cooking time: 20 min

Preparation:

Place the red pepper, garlic, parsley, mustard, onion Worcestershire sauce, lemon juice and olive oil in a food processor.

Place the fish, sauce and the rest of the vegetables in a large parchment baking bag. Bake at 190C fan/ gas 5 for 20 min then serve.

Nutritional value per serving: 225kcal, 33g protein, 12g carbs (3g fiber, 5g sugar), 5g fat (1g saturated), 11% calcium, 10% iron, 35% magnesium, 180% vitamin A, 77% vitamin C, 71% vitamin K, 13% vitamin B1, 19% vitamin B2, 51% vitamin B3, 14% vitamin B5, 34% vitamin B6, 15% vitamin B9, 25% vitamin B12.

38. Tray Bake Chicken

Quick, easy and tasty, this dish should be a summer staple in your kitchen since there is no shortage of fresh cherry tomatoes. The pesto adds a refreshing flavor to a simply seasoned chicken breast.

Ingredients (2 servings):

300g chicken breast

300g cherry tomatoes

2 tablespoons pesto

1 tablespoon olive oil

salt, pepper

Prep time: 5 min

Cooking time: 15 min

Preparation:

Place the chicken breast in a roasting tray, season, drizzle with the olive oil then grill for 10 min. Add the cherry tomatoes and grill for another 5 min until the chicken is cooked. Spread pesto over the top and serve next to the cherry tomatoes.

Nutritional value per serving: 312kcal, 36g protein, 7g carbs (2g fiber, 5g sugar), 19g fat (4g saturated), 15% magnesium, 25% vitamin A, 34% vitamin C, 11% vitamin E, 20% vitamin K, 10% vitamin B1, 88% vitamin B3, 13% vitamin B5, 33% vitamin B6.

39. Tofu burger

Tofu has all of the essential amino acids, and that makes it a perfect substitute for meat. The caramelized onions with chili flakes and Sriracha, paired with the teriyaki infused tofu will delight your taste buds.

Ingredients (1 serving):

85g tofu (extra firm)

1 tablespoon teriyaki marinade

1 tablespoon Sriracha

1 lettuce leaf

30g carrot, shredded

¼ red onion, sliced

½ teaspoon red chili flakes

1 medium-sized whole wheat roll

Prep time: 5 min

Cooking time: 10 min

Preparation:

Heat the grill.

Marinate the tofu in teriyaki marinade, red chili flakes and Sriracha then grill it for 3-5 min on each side.

Fry the red onion in a non-stick pan until caramelized.

Cut the roll in half until you can open it like a book. Stuff the roll with the grilled tofu, caramelized onion, carrots and lettuce and serve.

Nutritional value per serving: 194kcal, 11g protein, 28g carbs (5g fiber, 8g sugar), 5g fat (1g saturated), 21% calcium, 14% iron, 19% magnesium, 95% vitamin A, 10% vitamin B1, 14% vitamin B6.

40. Hot Cod

High in protein and healthy fats and low in carbs, this super spicy cod will give a jolt for the rest of your day. Serve it with a bit of brown rice if you need a carb boost for an evening workout and add 2 more peppers if you feel you can handle more spice.

Ingredients (2 servings):

340g white cod

10 cherry tomatoes, halved

2 jalapeno peppers, sliced

2 tablespoons olive oil

sea salt

chili powder

Prep time: 5 min

Cooking time: 10 min

Preparation:

Heat the oil in a non-stick pan. Coat the cod in salt and chili powder, add to the pan and cook for 10 min on medium heat. Toss in the peppers 1-2 min before the fish is cooked through.

Serve with cherry tomatoes.

Nutritional value per serving: 279kcal, 30g protein, 6g carbs (1g fiber, 1 g sugar), 16g fat (2g saturated), 11% magnesium, 17% vitamin A, 38% vitamin C, 26% vitamin E, 33% vitamin K, 24% vitamin B3, 43% vitamin B6, 26% vitamin B12.

41. Grilled Mushroom and Zucchini Burger

The Portobello mushrooms have a thick, meaty texture that makes them a favorite among vegetarians and meat lovers alike. Indulge in nature's burger and get a load of minerals and vitamins at a minimal calorie cost.

Ingredients (1 serving):

1 large portabella mushroom cap

¼ small zucchini, sliced

1 teaspoon roasted bell peppers

1 slice of low fat cheese

4 spinach leaves

olive oil spray

1 medium-sized whole wheat roll

Prep time: 5 min

Cooking time: 5 min

Preparation:

Heat the grill. Spray the mushroom cap with olive oil then grill both mushroom and zucchini slices.

Cut the roll in half, horizontally, then place the ingredients in layers on one half and cover with the other. Serve immediately.

Nutritional value per serving: 185kcal, 12g protein, 24g carbs (4g fiber, 5g sugar), 4g fat (1g saturated), 21% calcium, 17% iron, 20% magnesium, 78% vitamin A, 28% vitamin C, 242% vitamin K, 15% vitamin B1, 37% vitamin B2, 26% vitamin B3, 16% vitamin B5, 16% vitamin B6, 31% vitamin B9.

42. Mediterranean Fish

What better way to reach your daily B12 requirement than with a dish bursting of Mediterranean flavors? The rest of the vitamins and minerals are also well represented and the protein count is at a good amount for a light supper.

Ingredients (2 servings):

200g fresh trout

2 medium-sized tomatoes

3 teaspoons capers

½ red bell pepper, chopped

1 garlic clove, chopped

10 green olives, sliced

¼ onion, chopped

½ cup spinach

1 tablespoon olive oil

salt and pepper

Prep time: 10 min

Cooking time: 15 min

Preparation:

Heat a large pan over medium heat; add whole tomatoes, garlic and olive oil. Cover and let it simmer for a few minutes until the tomatoes begin to soften.

Add the onion, bell pepper, olives, capers, salt and pepper (and a little water if necessary). Cover and let it simmer until the tomatoes have broken down and the bell pepper and onion have softened.

Add the trout, cover and poach for 5-7 min.

Add the spinach at the last minute then serve.

Nutritional value per serving: 305kcal, 24g protein, 7g carbs (1g fiber, 4g sugar), 11g fat (3g saturated), 10% calcium, 12% magnesium, 36% vitamin A, 56% vitamin C, 62% vitamin K, 13% vitamin B1, 33% vitamin B3, 12% vitamin B5, 25% vitamin B6, 15% vitamin B9, 105% vitamin B12.

43. Vegan friendly dinner

A vegan friendly meal with a good amount of protein and vitamins. Give your palate the taste it deserves with this sweet and spicy sauce that flavors a filling amount of tofu and is easy to make.

Ingredients (2 servings):

340g tofu

¼ cup soy sauce

¼ cup brown sugar

2 teaspoons sesame oil

1 teaspoon olive oil

1 teaspoon chili flakes

2 garlic cloves, minced

1 teaspoon ginger, freshly grated

salt

Prep time: 5 min

Cooking time: 15 min

Preparation:

Mix the brown sugar, soy sauce, sesame oil, ginger, chili flakes and salt in a bowl and set aside.

Pour olive oil into a sauce pan and heat then fry the tofu for about 10 min.

Pour the sauce into the pan and cook for 3-5 min. Serve when the sauce has thickened and the tofu is done.

Nutritional value per serving: 245kcal, 17g protein, 15g carbs (1g fiber, 11g sugar), 15g fat (3g saturated), 34% calcium, 19% iron, 19% magnesium, 11% vitamin B2, 11% vitamin B6.

44. Tuna Melt

Unlike a regular tuna melt that is high in saturated fats and carbs, this one has a moderate amount of carbs and packs the protein-punch of a tuna can, making it an excellent meal that supports lean muscle growth.

Ingredients (2 servings):

1 can of tuna (165g)

2 slices of low-fat mozzarella cheese

2 teaspoons tomato sauce

1 whole wheat English muffin

a sprinkle of oregano

Prep time: 5 min

Cooking time: 3 min

Preparation:

Preheat the oven to 190C fan/ gas 5.

Slice the English muffin then smear each half with the tomato sauce. Top with the tuna, sprinkle with the oregano and place one slice of cheese on top of the tuna. Place the mini-melts in the oven and bake for 2-3 min or until the cheese has melted then divide between 2 plates and serve.

Nutritional value per serving: 255kcal, 31g protein, 14g carbs (2g fiber, 2 g sugar), 6g fat (4g saturated), 29% calcium, 11% iron, 13% magnesium, 10% vitamin B1, 10% vitamin B2, 60% vitamin B3, 23% vitamin B6, 52% vitamin B12.

45. Chicken with Avocado Salad

A meal that provides a great balance of quality protein and healthy fats that will keep you satisfied without overdoing it on the carbs front. Replace the vinegar with lemon juice for a fresher feel.

Ingredients (1 serving):

100g chicken breast

1 teaspoon smoked paprika

2 teaspoons olive oil

For the salad:

½ medium avocado, diced

1 medium tomato, chopped

½ small red onion, thinly sliced

1 tablespoon parsley, roughly chopped

1 teaspoon red wine vinegar

Prep time: 10 min

Cooking time: 10 min

Preparation:

Heat the grill to medium. Rub the chicken with 1 teaspoon olive oil and paprika. Cook for 5 min on each side until it is cooked through and lightly charred. Cut the chicken in thick slices.

Mix the salad ingredients together, season, add the rest of the olive oil and serve with the chicken.

Nutritional value per serving: 346kcal, 26g protein, 14g carbs (6g fiber, 4g sugar), 22g fat (3g saturated), 16% magnesium, 22% vitamin, 44% vitamin C, 18% vitamin E, 38% vitamin K, 12% vitamin B1, 11% vitamin B2, 66% vitamin B3, 19% vitamin B5, 43% vitamin B6, 22% vitamin B9.

SNACKS

1. Cherry Tomatoes with Cottage Cheese

Cut 5 cherry tomatoes in half and smear them with 2 tablespoons goat cheese mixed with fresh dill and a pinch of salt.

Nutritional value: 58kcal, 4g protein, 10g carbs, 30% vitamin A, 40% vitamin C, 20% vitamin K, 10% vitamin B1, 10% vitamin B6, 10% vitamin B9.

2. Avocado on Toast

Toast a small piece of whole wheat bread then cover it with 50g of mashed avocado and sprinkle with salt and pepper.

Nutritional value: 208kcal, 5g protein, 28g carbs (6g fiber, 2g sugar), 9g fat (1g saturated), 13% vitamin K, 13% vitamin B9.

3. Bell Peppers with Cottage Cheese

Cut a small bell pepper in half, deseed it then stuff it with 50g cottage cheese mixed with your choice of seasoning.

Nutritional value: 44kcal, 6g protein, 3g carbs (3g sugar), 49% vitamin C.

4. Rice Cake with Peanut Butter

Spread 1 rice cake with 1 tablespoon creamy peanut butter.

Nutritional value: 129kcal, 5g protein, 10g carbs (1g fiber, 1 g sugar), 8g fat (1g saturated), 10% vitamin B3.

5. Celery Sticks with Goat Cheese and Green Olives

Top 3 medium celery sticks with 3 tablespoons goat cheese and 3 sliced green olives.

Nutritional value: 102kcal, 4g protein, 6g carbs (3g fiber), 6g fat (4g saturated), 12% calcium, 45% vitamin K, 18% vitamin A, 12% vitamin B9.

6. Yogurt with Dried Goji Berries

Mix 150g low-fat yogurt with 10g goji berries.

Nutritional value: 134kcal, 7g protein, 19g carbs (1g fiber, 18% sugar), 4g fat (1g saturated), 27% calcium, 24% iron, 13% vitamin C, 19% vitamin B2, 13% vitamin B12.

7. Apple and Peanut Butter

Slice 1 small apple and spread 1 tablespoon creamy peanut butter on the pieces.

Nutritional value: 189kcal, 4g protein, 28g carbs (5g fiber, 20g sugar), 8g fat (1g saturated), 14% vitamin C, 14% vitamin B3.

8. Greek Yogurt with Strawberries.

Mix 150g Greek Yogurt with 5 medium-sized strawberries cut in half.

Nutritional value: 150kcal, 11g protein, 10g carbs (10g sugar), 8g fat (5g saturated), 10% calcium, 60% vitamin C.

9. Nut Mix

Mix together 10g walnuts, 10g almond and 30g raisins.

Nutritional value: 217kcal, 4g protein, 25g carbs (2g fiber, 17g sugar), 13g fat (1g saturated), 10% magnesium.

10. Ham and Celery Sticks

Wrap 6 medium celery sticks with 3 slices of ham and serve with 1 teaspoon of whole grain mustard.

Nutritional value: 129kcal, 15g protein, 6g carbs (6g fiber), 3g fat, 12% calcium, 24% vitamin A, 12% vitamin C, 90% vitamin K, 18% vitamin B1, 12% vitamin B2, 24% vitamin B3, 15% vitamin B6, 24% vitamin B9.

11. Yogurt with Tropical Fruit

Add 150g Greek Yogurt with ½ cup cut-up kiwi and ¼ cup cut-up mango.

Nutritional value: 210kcal, 12g protein, 25g carbs (2g fiber, 19g sugar), 8g fat (5g saturated), 13% calcium, 11% vitamin A, 155% vitamin C, 46% vitamin K.

12. Blueberry Yogurt

Blend 150g low fat yogurt with ½ cup blueberries.

Nutritional value: 136kcal, 8g protein, 21g carbs (2g fiber, 18g sugar), 3g fat (1g saturated), 27% calcium, 13% vitamin C, 18% vitamin K, 21% vitamin B2, 13% vitamin B12.

13. Cup of Popcorn

Nutritional value: 31kcal, 1g protein, 6g carbs (1g fiber).

14. Roasted Chickpeas

Nutritional value 50g: 96kcal, 4g protein, 13g carbs (4g fiber, 2g sugar), 3g fat.

BODYBUILDING SHAKE RECIPES

Day 1

Breakfast: All in one shake

Energy, Muscle Gain Shake

Preparation:

Mix all the ingredients together in a juicer or blender at high speed and then enjoy a delicious shake.

We all know how hard it is to gain muscle; we always need some help with this problem. So here is a great shake to improve muscle gain and also strengthen the body. You can drink it any time of the day, but we suggest breakfast as a good time.

Ingredients:

- Milk, 400 ml
- 2 scoops Whey Protein Powder
- 2 banana 140g
- Almond oil 2 tbsp.
- 1 apple

Nutrition facts:

- Calories: 443
- Proteins: 32.5 g
- Carbs: 45 g
- Fat: 16 g

Day 2

Lunch: Get big Shake

Muscle Gain Shake

Preparation:

Mix all the ingredients together in a juicer or blender at high speed and then enjoy a delicious shake.

Eat big to get big that is the secret to building large amounts of muscle mass based mainly on a high percentage of protein's. To reach that goal you have to put a lot of effort and eat right, here is a great shake to help you with this.

Ingredients:

- ½ cup unsweetened almond milk
- 2 tbsp. maple syrup
- 2 frozen bananas
- 1 scoop whey protein powder
- 3 tbsp. of almond butter

Nutritional facts:

- Calories – 830

- Total fat- 30g (healthy fat from almond butter)
- Carbs – 115g
- Fiber- 14g
- Net Carbs -101 g
- Gluten Free
- Protein: 46 g

Day 3

Breakfast: No powder Shake

Muscle gain shake

Preparation:

Mix all the ingredients together in a juicer or blender at high speed and then enjoy a delicious shake.

Get the most out of your mix with this great recipe. Running out of time, and yet you want to achieve your nutritional quota, this delicious drink is ready in less than a minute. Your body needs a protein rich milkshake "super" for your muscles that will give you a good balance of carbohydrates and protein and what better way to do this than with this mix of ingredients.

Ingredients:

- Almond oil 2 tbsp.
- 2 tbsp. Peanut Butter
- ½ - 1 tsp Honey
- 1 medium Banana
- 2 cups Milk
- 2 scoops Whey Protein powder

Nutrition Facts:

- Calories: 601
- Protein: 49 g
- Carbs: 63 g
- Fat: 25 g

Day 4

Breakfast: Coffee Protein Shake

Muscle Gain Shake

Preparation:

Mix all the ingredients together in a juicer or blender at high speed and then enjoy a delicious shake.

This shake recipe takes seconds to make, and will be a tasty one. Make sure you use all the ingredients, blend them well and serve it after a training session. Muscle gain is one of the hardest things to achieve at the gym, so any help you can get will definitely be worth the effort.

Ingredients:

- 2 scoops Whey Protein powder
- 8 ounces Coffee
- 8 ounces 2% Milk
- 2 tbsp. Caramel Creamer

Nutrition facts:

- Calories: 398

- Protein 58.4 g
- Carbs 13.4 g
- Fat 6.4 g

Day 5

Breakfast: Peanut Butter Bulking Protein Shake

Muscle Gain Shake

Preparation:

Mix all the ingredients together in a juicer or blender at high speed and then enjoy a delicious shake.

This shake recipe is a great one to improve your performance in the gym and to increase muscle growth. Place ingredients into a blender until smooth. You might also want to use whole milk and additional peanut butter to turn this protein shake into a higher calorie weight gainer, it's up to you.

Ingredients:

- 8 oz. skim milk
- 1 banana
- 1 tbsp. peanut butter
- 2 scoops of whey protein powder

Nutritional facts:

- Calories 498

- Protein 58 g
- Carbs 44.1 g
- Fat 11 g

Day 6

Breakfast: Pink Super Shake

Muscle Gain Shake

Preparation:

Mix all the ingredients together in a juicer or blender at high speed and then enjoy a delicious shake.

When it comes to massive weight increases, it's more important to consume the right amount of calories from a proper ratio of carbohydrates to protein so you have enough energy to train and enough protein to allow your muscles to develop.

Ingredients:

- ¾ cup organic frozen raspberries
- ½ small banana
- 1 scoop whey protein powder
- ½ tbsp. raw coconut butter
- 5 g glutamine
- 1 cup spring water

Nutritional facts:

- Calories: 268
- Protein : 16.5 g
- Carbs: 44.5 g
- Fat 6.7 g

Day 7

Breakfast: Banana Protein Shake

Muscle Gain Shake

Proteins are the most important nutrients for muscle growth. They ensure that the body functions properly. For practitioners of bodybuilding, they allow you to have bigger muscles provided, of course, you follow appropriate training, and you have a healthy diet. This is an easy-to-prepare shake that has a large amount of protein.

Preparation:

Mix all the ingredients together in a juicer or blender at high speed and then enjoy a delicious shake.

Ingredients:

- 8 oz. skim milk
- 1 banana
- ½ cups of oats
- 2 scoops of whey protein powder

Nutritional facts:

- Calories 554

- Protein 58g

- Carbs 67.5g

- Fat 6g

Day 8

Breakfast: Banana Berry Protein Shake

Gaining Mass Protein shake

This is a great shake for gaining strength and mass in a short period of time, with no delays. It's healthy, natural, and will make a big impact in your gym routine. So let's see the ingredients and all that it has to offer you.

Preparation:

Mix all the ingredients together in a juicer or blender at high speed and then enjoy a delicious shake.

Ingredients:

- 12 ounces of water
- 4 ice cubes
- 1 banana
- 2 scoops of whey protein

Nutritional facts:

- Calories 314

- Protein 45.1g
- Carbs: 32.1g
- Fat 2.4g

Day 9

Breakfast: Almond and Banana Thirst

Gaining Mass Shake

Increase your muscle gain using this shake recipe, and then track your progress the day after you've trained to see if it helped your performance. You could even prepare it the night before in order to make all the ingredients combine even better.

Preparation:

Mix all the ingredients together in a juicer or blender at high speed and then enjoy a delicious shake.

Ingredients:

- 1 frozen medium banana
- 1 cup plain yogurt
- 100 ml ice cold water
- 1 ounce ground almonds
- 1 cup raw oats

Nutritional facts:

- Calories: 650

- Protein: 53 g
- Carbs: 75 g
- Fat: 15 g

Day 10

Lunch: Cinnamon Protein Shake

Gaining Muscle Shake

Follow this shake recipe to increase your muscle gain, with a low fat intake. You can drink this shake any time of the day.

Preparation:

Mix all the ingredients together in a juicer or blender at high speed and then enjoy a delicious shake.

Ingredients:

- 1 cup Skim Milk
- 1 frozen Banana
- 1 scoop Whey Protein Powder
- 1 tbsp. Peanut Butter

Nutritional Facts:

- Calories: 391
- Protein: 38g
- Carbs: 42.1g
- Fat: 10g

Day 11

Breakfast: Heavy gainer Shake

Gaining Mass Shake

Here is a great shake recipe that will give you a huge boost of energy and also will help increasing your muscle development. So be ready for a great experience that will improve your gym sessions.

Preparation:

Mix all the ingredients together in a juicer or blender at high speed and then enjoy a delicious shake.

Ingredients:

- 10-14 oz. pure water
- 1/2 cup raw almonds
- 1/2 large frozen banana
- 2 scoops whey protein powder

Nutritional facts:

- Calories: 380
- Proteins: 75 g

- Carbs: 57 g
- Fat: 15 g

Day 12

Breakfast: Extreme Energy Shake

Gaining mass and energy Shake

If you were looking for something to supply you with some extra energy and also improve your muscle growth you should go for this shake recipe. This shake is full of healthy ingredients. Green Tea has been said to prevent cancer and flax seeds provide a good serving of omega 3 which is important for your body's development.

Preparation:

Mix all the ingredients together in a juicer or blender at high speed and then enjoy a delicious shake.

Ingredients:

- 10 oz. pure water
- 10 strawberries (Fresh or Frozen)
- 1 tbs. flax-seed oil
- 1/2 tsp Green Tea Powder
- 1/2 tsp vanilla extract
- 1 scoop Whey Protein Powder

Nutritional Facts:

- Calories: 420
- Protein: 50 g
- Carbs: 42 g
- Fat: 17 g

Day 13

Lunch: Peaches Shake

Gaining muscle Shake

The peaches in this shake give it a great flavor and cottage cheese is an excellent source of protein and is easy to digest. The best time of the day to drink this shake would be in the morning but you can drink it any time.

Preparation:

Mix all the ingredients together in a juicer or blender at high speed and then enjoy a delicious shake.

Ingredients:

- 8 oz. pure water
- 1 ripe peach
- 2 tbs. low-fat cottage cheese
- Brown sugar
- 1.5 scoop whey protein powder

Nutritional Facts:

- Calories: 250

- Proteins: 40 g
- Carbs: 21 g
- Fat: 8 g

Day 14

Breakfast: Blueberry Shake

Gaining muscle Shake

Let's start the day off with a great shake recipe that will maintain your energy levels high, and provide the required protein intake so you can increase more muscle in a shorter time period. Blueberries are known to be great antioxidants and help prevent cancer.

Preparation:

Mix all the ingredients together in a juicer or blender at high speed and then enjoy a delicious shake.

Ingredients:

- 10 oz. Pure water
- 1/2 cup fresh or frozen blueberries
- 1.5 scoop whey protein powder
- 2 tsp. flax-seed oil

Nutritional Facts:

- Calories: 210 g

- Proteins: 39g
- Carbs: 22 g
- Fat: 4 g

Day 15

Breakfast: Strawberry Shake

Gaining muscle Shake

There is no better way of getting fast results when trying to get muscle growth, than using shakes and this shake recipe will taste delicious because of the combination of strawberries and cottage cheese.

Preparation:

Mix all the ingredients together in a juicer or blender at high speed and then enjoy a delicious shake.

Ingredients:

- 10 oz. pure water
- 8 frozen strawberries
- 4 tbs. low-fat cottage cheese
- 1.5 scoop whey protein powder

Nutritional Facts:

- Calories: 310 g
- Proteins: 51g

- Carbs: 27g
- Fat: 7 g

Day 16

Breakfast: Banana delight Shake

Gaining muscle Shake

Combine the following ingredients to get a shake high in omega 3 and high in potassium to help you increase muscle gain, and also maintain a healthy body.

Preparation:

Mix all the ingredients together in a juicer or blender at high speed and then enjoy a delicious shake.

Ingredients:

- 8 oz. pure water
- 1/2 banana (frozen)
- 2 scoops whey protein powder
- 2 tsp. flax-seed oil

Nutritional Facts:

- Calories: 350 g
- Proteins: 65g
- Carbs: 29g

- Fat: 9 g

Day 17

Breakfast: Pineapple Shake

Gaining muscle Shake

Try this amazing shake recipe that is well known for fast results and delicious taste. It's perfect to help you increase your muscle gain, and will have a strong effect on your immune system.

Preparation:

Mix all the ingredients together in a juicer or blender at high speed and then enjoy a delicious shake.

Ingredients:

- 1 cup of pineapple juice
- 3 strawberries
- 1 banana
- 1 tsp. of yogurt
- 1 scoop whey protein powder

Nutritional Facts:

- Calories: 340 g
- Proteins: 63g

- Carbs: 27g
- Fat: 10 g

Day 18

Breakfast: Muscle Shake

Gaining muscle Shake

Having problems getting bigger muscles? If the answer is yes, you should try this shake recipe that will bring instant results in your training and energy throughout the day.

Preparation:

Mix all the ingredients together in a juicer or blender at high speed and then enjoy a delicious shake.

Ingredients:

- 1 c. low-fat milk
- 1/2 c. plain low-fat yogurt
- 1 banana, sliced
- 2 tbsp. Whey Protein Powder
- 6 strawberries, sliced
- 1 tsp. wheat germ
- 1 tbsp. honey or maple syrup
- 1/4 cup of any frozen berries

- Pinch of nutmeg or carob powder

Nutritional Facts:

- Calories: 600
- Proteins: 70g
- Carbs: 54g
- Fat: 15 g

Day 19

Breakfast: Oatmeal Shake

Gaining muscle Shake

This is a great shake recipe to increase muscle mass and protect your heart. It will help you stay alert during the entire day, go for it.

Preparation:

Mix all the ingredients together in a juicer or blender at high speed and then enjoy a delicious shake.

Ingredients:

- 2 scoops whey protein powder
- 1 cup sugar-free vanilla ice cream
- 1 cup oatmeal
- 2 cups non-fat milk
- 1.2 cup water
- A splash of peppermint extract!

Nutritional Facts:

- Calories: 621

- Proteins: 65g
- Carbs: 58g
- Fat: 22 g

Day 20

Lunch: Tropical Shake

Gaining muscle Shake

This is one of the most delicious shakes I have ever tasted and I am sure you will enjoy it. The mix between banana, pineapple, and coconut gives it a tropical flavor that should go well in the morning or mid-morning. The bananas don't have to be frozen, they can be room temperature but some people prefer that it be cold if they have just finished working out.

Preparation:

Mix all the ingredients together in a juicer or blender at high speed and then enjoy a delicious shake.

Ingredients:

- 8 oz. pure water
- 1/2 tsp. pineapple extract
- 1/2 tsp. coconut extract
- 1 tbsp. cottage cheese
- 1/2 frozen banana

185 Bodybuilding Meal and Shake Recipes to Make You Look Incredible

Nutritional Facts:

- Calories: 540
- Proteins: 25g
- Carbs: 43g
- Fat: 17g

Day 21

Lunch: Fruit Shake

Gaining muscle Shake

Protein is the key to muscle growth and recovery. Make sure you try this shake at any time of the day. This berry shake has many antioxidant qualities that will benefit you as you age and will prevent you from getting sick as often and that can be very important when you can't afford to take week long breaks from working out.

Preparation:

Mix all the ingredients together in a juicer or blender at high speed and then enjoy a delicious shake.

Ingredients:

- 2 scoops Milk protein powder
- 4 large strawberries
- blueberries (a small handful)
- water (just a few drops)
- 3 eggs

Nutritional Facts:

- Calories: 470
- Proteins: 45g
- Carbs: 39g
- Fat: 15g

Day 22

Breakfast: Apple Pie Delight Shake

Muscle gain Shake

Athletes who consume more protein will increase more muscle mass than sedentary people because they maximize growth potential so try to make sure you add this shake just before or just after a training session. The mixture of flavors from apple, cinnamon, and nutmeg give an original flavor not normally found in other shakes.

Preparation:

Mix all the ingredients together in a juicer or blender at high speed and then enjoy a delicious shake.

Ingredients:

- 1 scoop Whey protein powder
- 1 peeled and cored apple, cut into pieces
- 1 1/2 cups of milk
- 1/2 tsp cinnamon
- 1/2 tsp nutmeg
- 5 Ice Cubes

Nutritional Facts:

- Calories: 350
- Proteins: 35g
- Carbs: 21g
- Fat: 10g

Day 23

Breakfast: Pumpkin Shake

Low on carbs Shake

Here's one shake for you that's a great source of protein and provides a high level of energy during the day. The flax oil and yogurt provide you with several ingredients for your bodies overall function and help give this shake a boost of calcium and omega 3.

Preparation:

Mix all the ingredients together in a juicer or blender at high speed and then enjoy a delicious shake.

Ingredients:

- 2 Scoops Milk protein powder
- 8 oz. water
- 1 tbsp. Flax oil
- 1 tsp. Pumpkin pie spice
- 8 oz. Yogurt
- 4-6 ice cubes

Nutritional Facts:

- Calories: 300
- Proteins: 40g
- Carbs: 26g
- Fat: 11g

Day 24

Breakfast: Cinnamon Shake

Muscle gain Shake

This shake should be consumed early in the morning before a training session because it's a good energy provider and will also help accelerate muscle recovery.

Preparation:

Mix all the ingredients together in a juicer or blender at high speed and then enjoy a delicious shake.

Ingredients:

- 1 graham cracker
- 1/2 tsp cinnamon
- vanilla extract
- 12oz. water
- 4 Ice Cubes

Nutritional Facts:

- Calories: 280
- Proteins: 10g

- Carbs: 15g
- Fat: 5g

Day 25

Breakfast: Peanut Butter and Banana Shake

Muscle gain Shake

Peanut butter is a great source of protein and energy. Many athletes use peanut butter as a main source of energy before training or before competing. The banana and almond content improve the flavor and make it even more digestive.

Preparation:

Mix all the ingredients together in a juicer or blender at high speed and then enjoy a delicious shake.

Ingredients:

- 2 scoops Whey Protein Powder
- 100g almond slices
- 1 tbsp. peanut butter
- 500ml skim milk
- half banana
- 1 table-spoon honey

Nutritional Facts:

- Calories: 600
- Proteins: 55g
- Carbs: 35g
- Fat: 10g

Day 26

Breakfast: Super Mix Shake

Muscle gain Shake

Depending on your metabolism, you will adapt to some of the shakes better than others. For those of you who prefer a sweeter flavor in your shakes, this is a good choice. You can adapt certain ingredients to change the flavor to your preference like the caramel, hazelnuts, or vanilla yogurt.

Preparation:

Mix all the ingredients together in a juicer or blender at high speed and then enjoy a delicious shake.

Ingredients:

- 10 Ice Cubes
- 12 oz. fat-free milk
- 2 tbsp. fat free vanilla yogurt or Kefir
- 1 tbsp. reduced fat peanut butter
- 2 tbsp. spoon hazelnuts
- 1 tbsp. caramel ice cream topping

Nutritional Facts:

- Calories: 430
- Proteins: 23g
- Carbs: 20g
- Fat: 11g

Day 27

Breakfast: Lean mass Banana Shake

Muscle gain Shake

People who stick to a muscle gain diet or routine will benefit even more if they add muscle shakes because of the ease of preparation and because of how fast the body can absorb the protein and nutrients.

Preparation:

Mix all the ingredients together in a juicer or blender at high speed and then enjoy a delicious shake.

Ingredients:

- 1/2 frozen banana
- 2 tbsp. Whipping cream (heavy cream, not cream out of a can)
- 2 eggs
- 10-12 oz. water
- 4-6 ice cubes

185 Bodybuilding Meal and Shake Recipes to Make You Look Incredible

Nutritional Facts:

- Calories: 320
- Proteins: 18g
- Carbs: 15g
- Fat: 9g

Day 28

Lunch: Sweet Boost Shake

Muscle gain Shake

Here is a great example of a shake recipe that has very different ingredients, but combined they are a great source of protein and will increase your gym performance.

Preparation:

Mix all the ingredients together in a juicer or blender at high speed and then enjoy a delicious shake.

Ingredients:

- 1 medium to large banana
- 8 oz. light Milk
- 1 tbsp. Flaxseed and Almond Mixture
- 1 tsp Maple Syrup
- Few drops of vanilla essence/extract
- 3-4 cubes ice
- 1 tbsp. low-fat natural yogurt

Nutritional Facts:

- Calories: 450
- Proteins: 19g
- Carbs: 16g
- Fat: 10g

Day 29

Breakfast: Orange Shake

Muscle gain Shake

Let's start the day with an awesome shake to boost our immune system and help you increase more muscle. This recipe is high in vitamin C and potassium because of the strawberries and orange juice which will also allow your muscles to recover faster.

Preparation:

Mix all the ingredients together in a juicer or blender at high speed and then enjoy a delicious shake.

Ingredients:

- 8 oz. Orange Juice
- 4-5 ice cubes
- 1 tsp. Vanilla Extract
- ½ banana
- 2-3 frozen strawberries
- 2 tsp. honey

Nutritional Facts:

- Calories: 291
- Proteins: 15g
- Carbs: 12g
- Fat: 5g

Day 30

Breakfast: Almond Shake Blast

Muscle gain Shake

Plan on having a better digestion after having this shake with this combination of oatmeal, raisins, almonds, and peanut butter. The raisins give it a great flavor and the oatmeal gives it a different texture than other shakes.

Preparation:

Mix all the ingredients together in a juicer or blender at high speed and then enjoy a delicious shake.

Ingredients:

- 10-12 oz. of skim milk
- 1.2 cup of raw oatmeal
- 1.2 cup of raisins
- 12 shredded almonds
- 1 tbsp. of peanut butter.

Nutritional Facts:

- Calories: 380

- Proteins: 18g
- Carbs: 15g
- Fat: 12g

Day 31

Breakfast: Wild berry Shake

Muscle Gain Shake

Raspberries are known to be very high on vitamin C and antioxidants which many medical professionals suggest as an anti-cancer supplement to your normal day to day foods and meals. It's the perfect mixture for those who want to gain muscle mass and strength. You can replace an ordinary snack with this healthy drink that is not very high on protein but will help take a break from all the other high protein shakes you will be taking on a daily basis.

Preparation:

Mix all the ingredients together in a juicer or blender at high speed and then enjoy a delicious shake.

Ingredients:

- 8 raspberries
- 4 strawberries
- 15 blueberries
- 16 ounces non-fat milk
- 1/2 cup ice cubes

Nutritional Facts:

- Calories: 210
- Proteins: 9g
- Carbs: 10g
- Fat: 8g

Day 32

Breakfast: Peanut Banana Shake

Muscle Gain Shake

In terms of nutrition this shake is high on lean protein and complex carbs, so it will increase muscle growth and recovery. It will also give you an energy boost while your training if you drink it half hour before.

Preparation:

Mix all the ingredients together in a juicer or blender at high speed and then enjoy a delicious shake.

Ingredients:

- ½ cup Peanuts
- 1/2 Banana
- 1 Cup Skim Milk
- 1/4 Cup Quaker Oats
- 2 Ice Cubes
- Pinch of Salt

Nutritional Facts:

- Calories: 230
- Proteins: 18g
- Carbs: 12g
- Fat: 5g

Day 33

Breakfast: Carrot Pineapple Shake

Muscle Gain Shake

This shake might look a little strange for you guys, but believe me it's a good one for you and your body. You can remove or lower the portions for some of the ingredients depending on your preference as this mix is very different from some of the others.

Preparation:

Mix all the ingredients together in a juicer or blender at high speed and then enjoy a delicious shake.

Ingredients:

- 1 cup chocolate milk
- 3/4 c shredded carrots
- 10 frozen pineapple chunks
- 2 tsp unsweetened shredded coconut
- 1 tsp vanilla
- 1 tsp sweet cream
- 4 oz. Neufchatel Cheese or cream cheese

Nutritional Facts:

- Calories: 220
- Proteins: 21g
- Carbs: 13g
- Fat: 13g

Day 34

Lunch: Pumpkin Shake

Muscle Gain Shake

Great shake recipe to help you increase your muscle gain and strength with a very unique taste that makes it fun to drink while still consuming a decent amount of protein. It's the perfect supplement for muscle recovery and muscle gain.

Preparation:

Mix all the ingredients together in a juicer or blender at high speed and then enjoy a delicious shake.

Ingredients:

- 3/4 c. milk (whatever kind you like)
- 1/4 c. canned pumpkin
- 1 tbsp. Pumpkin Pie flavored syrup
- 1/2 tsp. pumpkin pie spice
- 10 ice cubes

Nutritional Facts:

- Calories: 235

- Proteins: 20g
- Carbs: 17g
- Fat: 1.5g

Day 35

Breakfast: Blueberry Apple Shake

Energy Boost Shake

Maintaining a high level of energy is the goal of this shake. It will also provide you with some lean proteins that will help you even if you're a bit tired that day or if you just want to push yourself harder that day.

Preparation:

Mix all the ingredients together in a juicer or blender at high speed and then enjoy a delicious shake.

Ingredients:

- 1/2 small apple cut into small pieces (with skin)
- 1/2 cup cherries (dark, sweet, pitted)
- 1/2 cup blueberries
- 4 tbsp. wheat germ
- ice cubes (if desired)
- 1/2 cup whey protein

Nutritional Facts:

- Calories: 300
- Proteins: 39g
- Carbs: 18g
- Fat: 5g

Day 36

Breakfast: Cherry Banana Energy Boost Shake

Two great tasting ingredients in one shake. Cherries and bananas are provide a great source of fiber that your body needs when taking in large portions of protein. Try this drink before any training session night or day.

Preparation:

Mix all the ingredients together in a juicer or blender at high speed and then enjoy a delicious shake.

Ingredients:

- 1/2 cup cherries (dark, sweet, pitted)
- 1/2 cup Banana
- 4 tbsp. wheat germ
- ice cubes (if desired)
- 1/2 cup whey protein

Nutritional Facts:

- Calories:300

- Proteins: 39g
- Carbs: 18g
- Fat: 5g

Day 37

Breakfast: Egg Mania Shake

Muscle Gain Shake

You can have a muscle gain shake recipe with no protein powder in it and still intake a good amount of protein. The chick peas give it a green color but don't really change the flavor at all. This is a great combination of proteins and carbs.

Preparation:

Mix all the ingredients together in a juicer or blender at high speed and then enjoy a delicious shake.

Ingredients:

- 4 egg whites
- 1/2 cup cottage cheese
- 1 banana
- 1/4 cup chick peas
- pineapple slices
- Coconut milk
- Coconut extract can be added
- ice cubes

Nutritional Facts:

- Calories: 280
- Proteins: 25g
- Carbs: 40g
- Fat: 4g

Day 38

Breakfast: High Protein Shake

Muscle Gain Shake

Increase your gym performance by increase the amounts of protein you have on a daily basis. This shake is high on protein and high on flavor.

Preparation:

Mix all the ingredients together in a juicer or blender at high speed and then enjoy a delicious shake.

Ingredients:

- 1/2 c water
- 1 scoop Whey Protein Powder
- 2 tbsp. Honey
- 1 tbsp. Smooth Peanut Butter
- 1/2 cup Ice

Nutritional Facts:

- Calories: 114
- Proteins: 34g

- Carbs: 5.2g
- Fat: 4.5g

Day 39

Breakfast: Fruit Mix Shake

Muscle Gain Shake

This shake recipe can easily replace your breakfast but this still have a healthy portion of food to nourish your body. It has a lot of the nutrients your body needs to have a good start in the morning. Protein and carbs are included in this recipe to give your energy and strength when training.

Preparation:

Mix all the ingredients together in a juicer or blender at high speed and then enjoy a delicious shake.

Ingredients:

- 1/2 banana chopped
- 1/2 cup of chopped strawberries
- 1 small apple
- 1 small plum
- 1 cup of chocolate milk
- 1 tbsp. of smooth peanut butter
- 1 scoop Whey Protein Powder

Nutritional Facts:

- Calories: 700
- Proteins: 46g
- Carbs: 90g
- Fat: 20g

Day 40

Breakfast: Choco Shake

Muscle Gain Shake

A great way of combining a dark chocolate bar with the right ingredients to obtain a shake that will increase your gym performance and muscle gain.

Preparation:

Mix all the ingredients together in a juicer or blender at high speed and then enjoy a delicious shake.

Ingredients:

- 1 dark chocolate bar
- 4 eggs
- 3 cups milk
- 1 scoop Whey Protein Powder

Nutritional Facts:

- Calories: 290
- Proteins: 45g
- Carbs: 37g

- Fat: 19g

Day 41

Breakfast: Taste of Everything Shake

Muscle Gain Shake

This shake recipe is an excellent source of protein and fiber your body needs. It's full of nutrients and vitamins that will you both bigger muscles and more energy when training to build more muscles.

Preparation:

Mix all the ingredients together in a juicer or blender at high speed and then enjoy a delicious shake.

Ingredients:

- Grapes, 4 grapes, seedless
- Blackberries, fresh, 0.5 grams
- Blueberries, fresh, 25 berries
- Strawberries, fresh, 0.5 grams
- Pineapple, fresh, 1 slice, thin (3-1/2" diameter x 1/2" thick
- Apples, fresh, 10 grams
- Yogurt, plain, low fat, 0.5 container (4 oz.)
- Kale, 0.5 grams

- Broccoli, fresh, 1 stalk
- Oranges, 0.5 grams
- 1 scoop Whey Protein Powder

Nutritional Facts:

- Calories: 280
- Proteins: 48g
- Carbs: 31g
- Fat: 4.2g

Day 42

Breakfast: Wake up Now Shake

Muscle Gain Shake

Here is how you should start the day, energy will be the defining word for this shake, but don't think it's not good for gaining muscle too, because you would be wrong.

Preparation:

Mix all the ingredients together in a juicer or blender at high speed and then enjoy a delicious shake.

Ingredients:

- 1 fresh banana, medium
- 2 servings (60 grs) oat flakes
- 1-2 tbsp. peanut butter, smooth style
- 1 cup (250 ml) yogurt, plain, low fat (0% - 1.5% mf)
- 0.5 tbsp. (or less) cinnamon, ground

Nutritional Facts:

- Calories: 650
- Proteins: 28g

- Carbs: 85g
- Fat: 10g

Day 43

Lunch: Mango Tango Shake

Muscle Gain Shake

This is a great shake you can add to other days so you can take two shakes per day since it is high on fiber and low on fat. This lean shake will help you fight any tiredness in the gym and will improve your performance.

Preparation:

Mix all the ingredients together in a juicer or blender at high speed and then enjoy a delicious shake.

Ingredients:

- 2 large strawberries, fresh or frozen
- 10 blueberries, fresh or frozen
- 1 cup Orange Juice
- 1/2 mango, fresh or frozen
- 1 scoop Milk Protein Powder

Nutritional Facts:

- Calories:250

- Proteins: 30.5g
- Carbs: 52g
- Fat: 8.4g

Day 44

Breakfast: Pineapple Tangerine Shake

Muscle Gain Shake

To gain muscle, there is no secret; you have to train and eat right! You will struggle if you don't have enough energy while training and that's why adding ingredients that will give you a boost when necessary will make all the difference when trying to build stronger muscles.

Preparation:

Mix all the ingredients together in a juicer or blender at high speed and then enjoy a delicious shake.

Ingredients:

- 1/2 cup Pineapple, frozen chunks
- 1/2 cup Tangerines, (mandarin oranges), canned
- 2 tsp. honey
- 1 scoop Whey Protein Powder

Nutritional Facts:

- Calories:150

- Proteins: 39g
- Carbs: 17g
- Fat: 11g

Day 45

Breakfast: Peanut Butter Apple Shake

Muscle Gain Shake

Shakes can be a great source of calories and energy which are necessary to increase muscle mass. This delicious shake recipe is made to help you increase your muscle gain and maintain a high level of energy.

Preparation:

Mix all the ingredients together in a juicer or blender at high speed and then enjoy a delicious shake.

Ingredients:

- 3/4 Cup plain or vanilla yogurt
- 2 tbsp. Peanut Butter
- 1 Banana
- 1/8 Cup milk
- 3/4 Cup ice
- 1 apple

Nutritional Facts:

- Calories: 440
- Proteins: 22g
- Carbs: 50g
- Fat: 19g

Day 46

Breakfast: Banana Super Shake

Muscle Gain Shake

Vanilla almond milk will make this a great protein shake. It promotes muscle mass growth without unbalancing your diet. You can reduce or eliminate the cinnamon to make it to your specific preference.

Preparation:

Mix all the ingredients together in a juicer or blender at high speed and then enjoy a delicious shake.

Ingredients:

- 1/2 cup vanilla almond milk
- 1/2 cup water
- 1/2 banana
- Dash of cinnamon
- 1 scoop of vanilla protein powder

Nutritional Facts:

- Calories:350

- Proteins: 43g
- Carbs: 25g
- Fat: 5g

Day 47

Breakfast: Dark Oat Power Shake

Muscle Gain Shake

The combination of dark chocolate, cottage cheese, and oatmeal will increase your muscle development, and get you that energy boost that you were looking for in the gym while improve digestion and strengthening your heart.

Preparation:

Mix all the ingredients together in a juicer or blender at high speed and then enjoy a delicious shake.

Ingredients:

- 1/2 cup of Cottage Cheese (or 1 cup Greek yoghurt)
- 1/2 - 1 cup water (depending on desired thickness) or milk
- 10g dark chocolate
- ½ cup raw oatmeal
- 1/2 banana
- 1 scoop Whey Protein Powder

Nutritional Facts:

- Calories:150
- Proteins: 40g
- Carbs: 20g
- Fat: 8g

Day 48

Breakfast: Milk Protein Shake

Muscle Gain Shake

To build and maintain your muscle mass you need to increase carbohydrates and protein so that you have the energy to work hard and the ingredients to allow your muscles to fully develop.

Preparation:

Mix all the ingredients together in a juicer or blender at high speed and then enjoy a delicious shake.

Ingredients:

- 1 scoop Milk protein powder
- 1/2 bananas
- 1/2 cup almond slices
- 8 oz milk
- 3 ice cubes

Nutritional Facts:

- Calories:335
- Proteins: 31g

- Carbs: 25g
- Fat: 18g

Day 49

Breakfast: Avocado Shake

Muscle Gain Shake

Protein shakes with vegetables are uncommon but should be more normal because of the value they bring to your diet and to your body. Avocado is considered by some as a "super food" and is great for your body.

Preparation:

Mix all the ingredients together in a juicer or blender at high speed and then enjoy a delicious shake.

Ingredients:

- 1/2 avocado
- 1 tbsp. shredded coconut
- 1 cup almond milk
- 1 scoop Whey Protein Powder

Nutritional Facts:

- Calories: 300
- Proteins: 35g

- Carbs: 20g
- Fat: 8g

Day 50

Breakfast: Very Berry Shake

Muscle Gain Shake

A complete berry and protein combination to improve muscle growth and recovery all in one shake. The taste is magnificent and the results are even better when you need to train hard and want to see results.

Preparation:

Mix all the ingredients together in a juicer or blender at high speed and then enjoy a delicious shake.

Ingredients:

- ½ cup strawberries
- ¼ cup mixed berries (raspberries, blueberries and blackberries)
- ¼ cup organic pomegranate juice
- ¼ cup organic grape juice
- handful sliced almonds for topping
- 1 scoop Whey Protein Powder

Nutritional Facts:

- Calories: 200
- Proteins: 31g
- Carbs: 19g
- Fat: 1g

FAT REDUCING CALENDAR

Week 1

Day 1:

Fruit and Nuts Yogurt

Egg Drop Soup with Chicken and Noodles

Mushroom Pilaf with Lemon

Day 2:

Egg and Veggie Breakfast Bakes

Turkey Stir Fry

Stuffed Eggplant

Day 3:

Breakfast Guacamole

Lemmon-rubbed Barbecued Salmon

Orange, Walnut and Blue Cheese Salad

Day 4:

Fitness Smoothie

Chicken and Corn Salad

Veggie Red Curry

Day 5:

Banana Oatmeal Pancakes

Tangy Trout

Stuffed Zucchinis

Day 6:

Tuna on Toast

Garlic Beef

Fruit Salad

Day 7:

Bacon and Brie Omelette with Salad

Rice and Tomato Soup

Smoked Trout with Beetroot, Fennel and Apple Salad

Week 2

Day 1:

Berry Smoothie

Lemon Spaghetti with Broccoli and Tuna

Devilled Mushrooms

Day 2:

Spring Onion and Turkey Wraps

Chicken with Mushrooms

Mexican Rice and Bean Salad

Day 3:

Poached Eggs with Smoked Salmon and Spinach

Bean and Pepper Chili

Thai Vegetable and Coconut Milk Broth

Day 4:

Hummus with Pita Bread and Vegetables

Grilled Fish with Moroccan Spiced Tomatoes

Lentil, Carrot and Orange Soup

Day 5:

Oatmeal with Apples and Raisins

Spicy Seafood Stew

Chickpeas and Spinach Curry

Day 6:

Feta and Semi-dried Tomato Omelette

Spinach and Dates Stuffed Chicken

Roasted Carrots with Pomegranate and Blue Cheese

Day 7:

Fruit and Nuts Yogurt

Prawn Curry

Mexican Rice and Bean Salad

Week 3

Day 1:

Bacon and Brie Omelette with Salad

Bean and Pepper Chili

Tangy Trout

Day 2:

Fitness Smoothie

Garlic Beef

Stuffed Eggplant

Day 3:

185 Bodybuilding Meal and Shake Recipes to Make You Look Incredible

Breakfast Guacamole

Turkey Stir Fry

Fruit Salad

Day 4:

Egg and Veggie Breakfast Bakes

Lemon-rubbed Barbecued Salmon

Veggie Red Curry

Day 5:

Banana Oatmeal Pancakes

Egg Drop Soup with Chicken and Noodles

Smoked Trout with Beetroot, Fennel and Apple Salad

Day 6:

Tuna on Toast

Rice and Tomato Soup

Stuffed Zucchinis

Day 7:

Berry Smoothie

Chicken and Corn Salad

Orange, Walnut and Blue Cheese Dressing

Week 4

Day 1:

Oatmeal with Apples and Raisins

Lemon Spaghetti with Broccoli and Tuna

Lentil, Carrot and Orange Soup

Day 2:

Poached Eggs with Smoked Salmon and Spinach

Chicken with Mushrooms

Chickpeas and Spinach Curry

Day 3:

Spring Onion and Turkey Wraps

Spicy seafood Stew

Roasted Carrots with Pomegranate and Blue Cheese

Day 4:

Feta and Semi-dried Tomato Omelette

Bean and Pepper Chili

Fruit Salad

Day 5:

Hummus with Pita Bread and Vegetables

Prawn Curry

Mexican Rice and Bean Salad

Day 6:

Fruit and Nuts Yogurt

Spinach and Dates Stuffed Chicken

Thai Vegetable and Coconut Broth

Day 7:

Breakfast Guacamole

Tangy trout

Stuffed Eggplant

2 extra days for a full month:

Day 1:

Fitness Smoothie

Chicken and Corn Salad

Orange, Walnut and Blue Cheese Salad

Day 2:

Tuna on Toast

Turkey Stir Fry

Veggie Red Curry

FAT REDUCING MEAL RECIPES

BREAKFAST

1.   Feta and Semi-dried Tomato Omelette

A really quick, simple, low calorie recipe that will give your day the kick start it deserves. For an extra pinch of flavor, use tomatoes that have been preserved in a mixture of olive oil and Italian herbs.

Ingredients (1 serving):

2 eggs, lightly beaten

25g feta cheese, crumbled

4 semi-dried tomatoes, roughly chopped

1 teaspoon olive oil

mixed salad leaves, for serving

Prep time: 5 min

Cooking time: 5 min

Preparation:

Heat the oil in a small, non-stick frying pan, then add the eggs and cook, swirling them with a wooden spoon. When the eggs are a bit runny in the middle, add the tomatoes and feta, then fold the omelet in half. Cook for 1 min, then slide it onto a plate and serve with a mix of leaf salad.

Nutritional value per serving: 300kcal, 18g protein, 20g fat (7 saturated), 5g carbs (1g fiber, 4g sugar), 1.8g salt, 15% calcium, 22% vitamin D, 20% vitamin A, 15% vitamin C, 25% vitamin B12.

2. Oatmeal with Apples and Raisins

A warm, filling, calcium rich breakfast that is easy on the stomach and perfect as a pre-workout meal, due to its high carb content. Sprinkle with some cinnamon for a sweet, woody fragrance.

Ingredients (2 servings):

50g oats

250ml low-fat milk

2 apples, peeled and diced

50g raisins

½ tablespoon honey

Prep time: 5min

Cooking time: 10 min

Preparation:

Bring the milk to a boil in a saucepan over medium heat and stir with the oats for 3 minutes. When the concoction becomes creamy, add the apples and the raisins and boil for another 2min. Ladle the mix into 2 bowls, add the honey and serve immediately.

Nutritional value per serving: 256kcal, 9g protein, 2g fat (1g saturated), 47g carbs (4g fiber, 34g sugar), 17% calcium, 11% iron, 17% magnesium.

3. Hummus with Pita Bread and Vegetables

This is a simple and nutritious breakfast that you can quickly assemble in the morning and pack to work. The hummus stays in the fridge and the vegetables can be stuffed into the pita bread, making an easy to grab sandwich.

Ingredients (2 servings):

1 200g can of chickpeas, drained

1 clove of garlic, crushed

25g of tahini

¼ teaspoon cumin

lemon juice, squeezed from ¼ lemon

salt, pepper

3 tablespoons water

2 whole wheat pita bread

200g vegetable mix (carrots, celery, cucumber)

Prep time: 15 min

No cooking

Preparation:

Combine chickpeas, garlic, tahini, cumin, lemon juice, salt, pepper and water in a food processor and pulse several times until the mix becomes creamy.

Serve with toasted pita bread and vegetable mix.

Nutritional value per serving: 239kcal, 9g protein, 9g fat (1g saturated), 28g carbs (6g fiber, 4g sugar), 1,1g salt, 27% iron, 23% magnesium, 14% vitamin B1.

4. Spring Onion and Turkey Wraps

What better way to use leftover turkey bits, than to make a quick delicious tortilla sandwich? Give yourself a treat that is high in protein, low in saturated fat and flavored with the zesty taste of basil.

Ingredients (2 servings):

130g cooked turkey (boiled or roasted), shredded

3 spring onions, shredded

1 chunk of cucumber, shredded

2 curly lettuce leaves

1 tablespoons light mayonnaise

1 tablespoon pesto

2 whole wheat flour tortillas

Prep time: 5mins

No cooking

Preparation:

Mix together the pesto and mayonnaise. Divide the turkey, spring onions, cucumber and lettuce leaves between the 2 tortillas. Drizzle over the pesto dressing, wrap everything up and serve.

Nutritional value per serving: 267kcal, 24g protein, 9g fat (2g saturated), 25g carbs (2g fiber, 3g sugar), 1.6g salt, 34% vitamin B3, 27% vitamin B6.

5. Berry Smoothie

What better way to get half a day's worth of calcium than with this creamy yogurt based meal? Add some fibers and make it even more nutritional, by saving half the berries from the blender and tipping them over when the smoothie is done.

Ingredients (2 servings):

450g frozen berries

450g low fat yogurt

100ml low fat milk

25g porridge oats

1 teaspoon honey (optional)

Prep time: 10 min

No cooking

Preparation:

Mix the berries, yogurt and milk in a food processor until smooth. Then add and stir the porridge oats and pour into 2 glasses. Serve with a bit of honey.

Nutritional value per serving: 234kcal, 16g protein, 2g fat (2g saturated), 36g carbs (14g sugar), 45% calcium, 11% magnesium, 18% vitamin B2, 21% vitamin B12.

6. Poached Eggs with Smoked Salmon and Spinach

A filling, high-protein breakfast that will give your day a very satisfying start. You will have no problem reaching your daily requirement of vitamin A and your heart will thank you for the hearty amount of omega-3 fatty acids.

Ingredients (1 serving):

2 eggs

100g spinach, chopped

50g smoked salmon

1 tablespoon white vinegar

a little butter for spreading

1 piece of whole wheat bread, toasted

Prep time: 5 min

Cooking time: 20 min

Preparation:

Heat a non-stick frying pan, add the spinach and stir for 2 min.

In order to poach the eggs, bring a pan of water to the boiling point, add the vinegar and then lower the heat so that the water is simmering. Stir the water until you have a slight whirlpool then slide the eggs one by one. Cook each for about 4 minutes then remove the egg with a slotted spoon.

Butter the piece of toast then put the spinach on it, the smoked salmon and the eggs. Season as needed and serve.

Nutritional value per serving: 349kcal, 31g protein, 19g fat (6g saturated), 13g carbs (4g fiber, 2g sugar), 3.6g salt, 23% iron, 23% magnesium, 197% vitamin A, 46% vitamin C, 21% vitamin D, 15% vitamin B6, 18% vitamin B12.

7. Bacon and Brie Omelette with Salad

A tasty omelette for those who prefer starting the day with a healthy filling of eggs and protein. Cut the omelette into wedges for a frittata look and savor with a salad instead of bread to cut back on the calories.

Ingredients (2 servings):

3 eggs, lightly beaten

100g smoked lardoons

50g brie, sliced

a small bunch of chives, chopped

1 tablespoon olive oil

½ teaspoon red wine vinegar

½ teaspoon Dijon mustard

½ cucumber, halved and deseeded

100g radishes, quartered

Prep time: 5 min

Cooking time 15 min

Preparation:

Heat 1 teaspoon in a small pan, add the lardoons and fry until crisp, then take it out of the pan and let it drain on kitchen paper.

Heat 1 teaspoon of the oil in a non-stick frying pan, then mix together the lardoons, eggs and some ground pepper. Pour into the frying pan and cook over low heat until it is almost done, then add the Brie and grill until it is set and golden.

Mix the remaining olive oil, vinegar, seasoning and mustard in a bowl and toss the radishes and cucumber. Serve alongside the omelette.

Nutritional value per serving: 395kcal, 25g protein, 31g fat (12g saturated), 3g carbs (2g fiber, 3g sugar), 2.2g salt, 10% vitamin A, 13% vitamin C, 15% vitamin D, 13% vitamin B12.

8. Fitness smoothie

A dairy-free vegan smoothie with pomegranate juice that will energize you for work or sustain your workout. You can add a tablespoon of ground flaxseeds for another 2g of fiber at the low cost of an extra 37kcal.

Ingredients (1 serving):

125ml soya milk

150ml pomegranate juice

30g tofu

1 large banana, cut into chunks

1 teaspoon honey

1 tablespoon almond

2 ice cubes

Prep time: 5 min

No cooking

Preparation:

Blend the soya milk and pomegranate juice with 2 ice cubes until the ice has broken down.

Add the banana, honey and tofu and blend until smooth, then pour the mix into a glass and sprinkle it with the flaked almonds.

Nutritional value per serving: 366kcal, 10g protein, 12g fat (1g saturated), 55g carbs (4g fiber, 50g sugar), 13% calcium, 11% iron, 15% magnesium, 14% vitamin C, 25% vitamin B6.

9. Tuna on Toast

A really quick, low calorie recipe that delivers a high amount of neuron protective B12. If you want an energy boost, spread the paste on a piece of whole wheat bread at about 120kcal per piece and serve with the bell pepper on the side.

Ingredients (4 servings):

2 cans of tuna in water (185g), half drained

3 hard-boiled eggs

1 spring onion, finely chopped

5 small pickles, diced

salt, pepper

4 bell peppers, halved, with the seeds cleaned

Prep time: 5 min

Cooking time: 10 min

Preparation:

Combine the tuna, eggs, spring onion, pickles and seasoning in a food processor and mix until smooth.

Fill the halves of the bell peppers with the composition and serve.

Nutritional value per serving: 240kcal, 23g protein, 8g fat (2g saturated), 4g carbs (1g fiber, 2g sugar), 14% magnesium, 47% vitamin A, 28% vitamin B6, 142% vitamin B12,.

10.   Banana Oatmeal Pancakes

Enjoy this healthier version of pancakes that replaces plain flower with rolled oats. The banana makes for a subtle sugar substitute, but you can also spread 1 teaspoon of honey (23kcal per teaspoon) if you feel like it.

Ingredients (8 pancakes):

50g rolled oats

4 eggs, lightly beaten

2 bananas, cut into chunks

½ teaspoon cinnamon

1 teaspoon olive oil for each pancake

Prep time: 5 min

Cooking time: 30 min

Preparation:

Combine all the ingredients in a food processor. Heat a non-stick frying pan, add a teaspoon of oil and drop ¼ cup of mix into the pan. Cook on each size until the pancake become lightly brown.

Nutritional value per pancake: 135kcal, 4g protein, 13g fat (3g saturated), 10g carbs (1g fiber, 3g sugar).

11. Breakfast Guacamole

You can't miss with a meal that contains avocado. High in healthy fats and fiber, with a smooth texture and a flavor richly enhanced by a bit of lemon juice, this breakfast guacamole will energize you till lunch.

Ingredients (2 servings):

1 ripe avocado

1 large tomato, roughly chopped

1 spring onion, finely chopped

1 clove of garlic crushed

lemon juice, from ½ lemon

salt

ground black pepper

2 slices of whole wheat bread, toasted

Prep time: 5 min

No cooking

Preparation:

Slice the avocado in half, lengthwise, then scoop out the pulp with a spoon and put it into a large bowl. Mash it up with a fork. Pour the lemon juice over the pulp and add the chopped tomato, the spring onion and garlic. Season with salt and lots of black pepper. Mix it around, spread it on a piece of toast and serve immediately.

Nutritional value per serving: 280kcal, 9g protein, 13g fat (2g saturated), 30g carbs (9g fiber, 5g sugar), 10% iron, 17% magnesium, 14% vitamin A, 29% vitamin C, 17% vitamin B6.

12. Egg and Veggies Breakfast Bakes

An inventive, easy to make breakfast that bakes an egg instead of frying it, saving you a substantial amount of saturated fats. The eggs make it filling, while the veggies are not only tasty but also loaded with vitamin A and C.

Ingredients (1 serving):

2 large field mushrooms

2 medium-sized tomatoes, halved

100g spinach

2 eggs

1 garlic clove, thinly sliced

1 teaspoon olive oil

Prep time: 5 min

Cooking time: 30 min

Preparation:

Heat the oven to 200C fan/gas 6. Put in the tomatoes and mushrooms into an ovenproof dish. Add the garlic, drizzle the oil and seasoning and then bake for 10 min.

Put the spinach in a large pan then pour over a kettle of boiling water to wilt it. Squeeze out the excess water and then add the spinach to the dish. Make a little gap between the veggies and crack the eggs into the dish. Cook for another 10 min in the oven until the eggs are done.

Nutritional value per serving: 254kcal, 18g protein, 16g fat (4g saturated), 16g carbs (6g fiber, 10g sugar), 31% iron, 17% calcium, 29% magnesium, 238% vitamin A, 11% vitamin D, 102% vitamin C, 18% vitamin B1, 51% vitamin B2, 20% vitamin B3, 29% vitamin B6, 22% vitamin B12.

13. Fruit and Nuts Yogurt

A great alternative to cereal, this high-carb breakfast will keep you full till lunch and give you the energy start you require to tackle your tasks. The mix of nuts delivers a substantial amount of healthy fats, while the yogurt makes sure that you get half a day's worth of calcium.

Ingredients (1 serving):

1 medium-sized banana, sliced

100g blueberries (fresh or frozen and defrosted)

20g walnuts

20g hazelnuts

10g raisins

200g fat free yogurt

Prep time: 5 min

No cooking

Preparation:

Mix the fruit with the nuts, layer up in a bowl with yogurt and serve.

Nutritional value per serving: 450kcal, 13g protein, 25g fat (2g saturated), 54g carbs (9g fiber, 32g sugar), 44% calcium, 16% magnesium, 30% vitamin C, 36% vitamin B6.

LUNCH

14. Egg Drop Soup with Chicken and Noodles

A quick and easy to make dish, perfect for a midday meal. The noodles contain enough energy boosting carbs that will sustain your throughout the day and the meat is loaded with vitamin B.

Ingredients (2 servings):

1 skinless, boneless chicken breasts, diced

1 egg, beaten

0.6l chicken soup

1 spring onion, finely chopped

70g whole wheat noodles

70g frozen sweet corn, or baby corn, halved lengthways

lemon juice

¼ teaspoon sherry vinegar

Prep time: 10 min

Cooking time: 15 min

Preparation:

Place the chicken and the soup in a large pan and bring to a simmer for 5 min. The noodles are to be cooked following the instructions on the pack.

Add the corn and boil for 2 min. Stir the broth and while it is still churning, hold a fork over the pan and pour the eggs over the prongs in a slow stream. Stir again in the same direction and then take it off the heat. Add the lemon juice and the vinegar.

Drain the noodles and divide them between 2 bowls. Pour the broth, scatter with the chopped onions and serve.

Nutritional value per serving: 273kcal, 26g protein, 6g fat (1g saturated), 30g carbs (3g fiber, 2g sugar), 1g salt, 96% vitamin B3, 42% vitamin B6.

15. Chicken and Corn Salad

A paprika-spiced chicken, served with grilled sweet corn and fresh, crisp lettuce, makes for a healthy, speedy salad, with copious amounts of vitamin B. The garlic based dressing tops an already tasty meal.

Ingredients (2 servings):

2 small skinless chicken breasts

1 corn cob

2 little gem lettuces, quartered lengthways

½ cucumber, diced

1 garlic cloves, crushed

1 tablespoon olive oil

1 teaspoon paprika

lemon juice, from half a lemon

salad dressing (2 servings):

1 clove garlic, crushed

75ml curd milk

1 tablespoon white wine vinegar

Prep time: 20 min

Cooking time: 20 min

Preparation:

Cut the chicken breasts lengthways in half so you are left with 4 chicken strips. Mix the paprika, garlic, 1 teaspoon oil and lemon juice with some seasoning and marinate the chicken for at least 20 min.

Heat a pan, add the remaining oil and cook the chicken for 3-4 min on each side until it is cooked through. Brush over the remaining oil and griddle the corn for about 5 min or until lightly charred. Make sure to cook evenly. Remove the corn cobs and cut off the kernels.

Combine the ingredients for the dressing.

Mix the cucumber and lettuce, put the chicken and corn on top and drizzle the dressing.

Nutritional value per serving : 253kcal, 29g protein, 8g fat (1g saturated), 14g carbs (3g fiber, 6g sugar), 20% iron, 40% magnesium, 96% vitamin B3, 72% vitamin B6.

16. Lemon Spaghetti with Broccoli and Tuna

15 minutes is all you need to whip up this zesty fish pasta that packs a significant energy punch. The mix of spaghetti, tuna and vegetable make this an all-round nutritious dish.

Ingredients (2 servings):

180g whole wheat spaghetti

100g can tuna in oil, drained

125g broccoli, cut into florets

40g pitted green olives, quartered

1 tablespoon capers, drained

juice and zest from ½ lemon

1 teaspoon olive oil, plus extra for drizzling

Prep time: 5 min

Cooking time: 10 min

Preparation:

Boil the spaghetti according to the instructions on the pack. 6 min in, add the broccoli and boil for 4 min or more until both are tender.

Mix the olives, shallots, capers, tuna, lemon zest and juice in a big bowl. Drain the pasta and broccoli, add to the bowl, mix well with the olive oil and black pepper and serve.

Nutritional value per serving: 440kcal, 23g protein, 11g fat (2g saturated), 62g carbs (5g fiber, 4g sugar), 1.4g salt, 12% iron, 20% magnesium, 25% vitamin A, 50% vitamin B3, 25% vitamin B6, 90% vitamin B12.

17. Lemon-rubbed Barbecued Salmon

Rich in healthy fats, protein and B vitamins, salmon is a fish that definitely deserves a spot on you plate. Serve with a simple mix of tomato and green salad to savor the fine taste of this lemony meal.

Ingredients (2 servings):

2*150g boneless salmon fillets

juice and zest ½ lemon

10g fresh tarragon, finely chopped

1 garlic clove, finely chopped

1 tablespoon oil

Prep time: 5 min

Cooking time: 10 min

Preparation:

Stir the lemon zest and juice, garlic, tarragon and olive oil in a dish, season with salt and pepper and then add the salmon fillets. Rub the mixture on the fish, cover and set aside for 10 min.

Heat the grill to high, remove the salmon fillets from the marinade, put them on a baking shit and grill for 7-10 min. Served when the salmon is just cooked through.

Nutritional value per serving: 322kcal, 31g protein, 22g fat (4g saturated), 1g carbs, 12% vitamin B2, 30% vitamin B1, 60% vitamin B3, 45% vitamin B6, 79% vitamin B12.

18. Rice and Tomato Soup

A hearty main course, the rice and tomato soup is a great way to take advantage of the fresh and savory tomatoes available in summer. You can also serve it cold, for a refreshing effect.

Ingredients (2 servings):

70g brown rice

200g tomatoes, chopped

1 teaspoon tomato puree

1 spring onion, finely chopped

1 small carrot, finely chopped

½ celery stick, finely chopped

½ l vegetable stock made with 1 cube

1 teaspoon golden caster sugar

1 teaspoon vinegar

a few parsley leaves, chopped

a few drops of pesto, to serve (optional)

Prep time: 10 min

Cooking time: 35 min

Preparation:

Heat the oil in a large pan, add the carrot, celery and onion and cook on medium heat until softened. Add the vinegar and sugar, cook for 1 min and then stir through the tomato puree. Add the tomatoes, the vegetable stock and the brown rise, cover and simmer for 10 min.

Divide into 2 bowls, and sprinkle some parsley, season. Add pesto if wanted.

Nutritional value per serving: 213kcal, 6g protein, 3g fat (1g saturated), 39g carbs (4g fiber, 13g sugar), 1.6g salt, 16% vitamin A, 22% vitamin C.

19. Spinach and Dates Stuffed Chicken

High in protein, with a balanced amount of carbs and lots of vitamins, this healthy meal covers pretty much everything, from nutrients to taste. The date and spinach stuffing add a welcomed sweetness.

Ingredients (2 servings):

2 boneless and skinless chicken breasts

100g spinach, chopped

1 small onion, finely chopped

1 garlic clove, finely chopped

4 dates, finely chopped

1 tablespoon pomegranate juice or honey

1 teaspoon cumin

1 tablespoon olive oil

100g frozen green beans

Prep time: 10 min

Cooking time: 15 min.

Preparation:

Heat the oven to 200C fan/gas 6. Heat the oil in a non-stick pan, add the onion, garlic and a dash of salt and cook for 5 min before adding the dates, spinach and ½ of the cumin. Cook for another 1-2 min.

Cut the chicken breasts in half, lengthways, and leave a part intact so as to be able to open them like a book. Stuff the chicken breasts and put them in an oven pan, add the rest of the cumin and seasoning, sprinkle with the honey or pomegranate juice and bake for 20 min. Serve with the frozen green peas, slightly steamed.

Nutritional value per serving: 257kcal, 36g protein, 4g fat (1g saturated), 21g carbs (3g fiber), 17% iron, 23% magnesium, 97% vitamin A, 36% vitamin C, 96% vitamin B3, 49% vitamin B6.

20. Bean and Pepper Chili

A healthy vegetarian midday meal with a spicy kick, this dish is a great way of getting 1/2 – 1/3 of your daily required amount of fiber. You can serve topped on a small portion of boiled brown rice with around 170kcal added to your meal.

Ingredients (2 servings):

170g peppers, deseeded and sliced

200g can kidney beans in chili sauce

200g can black beans, drained

200g tomatoes, chopped

1 small onion, chopped

1 teaspoon cumin

1 teaspoon chili powder

1 teaspoon sweet smoked paprika

1 teaspoon olive oil

Prep time: 15 min

Cooking time: 30 min

Preparation:

Heat the oil in a large pan, add the onion and pepper and cook for 8-10 min until softened. Add the spices and cook for 1 min.

Tip the beans and tomatoes, bring to a boil and simmer for 15 min. When the chili has thickened season and serve.

Nutritional value per serving: 183kcal, 11g protein, 5g fat (1g saturated), 26g carbs (12g fiber, 12g sugar), 16% iron, 14% magnesium, 16% vitamin A, 22% vitamin C, 14% vitamin B1.

21. Garlic Beef

Enjoy a quickly made beef steak that is not only high in protein and low in fat and carbs, but also loaded with vitamin B. Pair it with some cherry tomatoes for a filling and refreshing meal.

Ingredients (2 servings):

300g well-trimmed beef skirt

3 garlic cloves

2 tablespoons red wine vinegar

1 teaspoon black peppercorn

200g cherry tomatoes, halved with a splash of vinegar

Prep time: 10 min

Cooking time: 15min

Preparation:

Crush the peppercorns and garlic with a pinch of salt in a pestle and mortar until you have a slightly smooth paste, then stir in the vinegar. Sit the beef in dish, then rub the paste all over. Leave in the fridge for 2 hours.

Place a griddle pan over a very hot heat. Rub the marinade off the meat, add more salt. Cook the meat for about 5 min until charred on each side (make sure the cut is not too thick). Lift the meat onto a chopping board, then rest for 5 min before carving it into slices. Serve with cherry tomatoes.

Nutritional value per serving: 223kcal, 34g protein, 6g fats, 7g carbs (1g fiber, 3g sugar), 22% iron, 16% vitamin A, 22% vitamin C, 27% vitamin B2, 42% vitamin B3, 30% vitamin B6, 64% vitamin B12.

22. Grilled Fish with Moroccan Spiced Tomatoes

A sea bream based meal makes for an excellent source of protein. The South African sauce with its aromatic spices compliments its taste and it also goes well with sardines and sea bass.

Ingredients (2 servings):

2*140g skinless sea bream fillets

3 large tomatoes

1 ½ large red peppers, deseeded and halved

2 garlic cloves, crushed

20ml olive oil

1 teaspoon cumin

1 teaspoon ground paprika

1/8 teaspoon black pepper

a pinch of cayenne

small bunch parsley, roughly chopped

small bunch coriander, roughly chopped

Prep time: 30 min

Cooking time: 15 min

Preparation:

Heat the grill to high, place the peppers skin side up on a baking tray and place under the grill until black and blistered. Place in a bowl covered tightly and let them cool. When they are cool, remove the burnt skins then cut them into small pieces.

Skin the tomatoes, then cut into quarters, discard the seeds and dice.

Heat the oil in a large pan, add the garlic, the ground pepper and the spices and cook for 2 min. Add the peppers and tomatoes and cook over medium heat until the tomatoes are very soft. Smash the soft tomatoes and continue cooking until the liquid is reduced to sauce.

Heat the grill to high, place the fish on a baking tray lined with lightly oiled foil. Season and grill for 4-5 min until cooked through. Divide the sauce between plates place the fish on top and serve with the chopped herbs.

Nutritional value per serving: 308kcal, 25g protein, 18g fat (2g saturated), 16g carbs (4g fiber, 12 g sugar), 23%

magnesium, 45% vitamin A, 55% vitamin C, 12% vitamin B1, 12% vitamin B2, 14% vitamin B3, 34% vitamin B6.

23. Prawn Curry

You only need 20 min to make this delicious, curry flavored seafood dish. The creamy, aromatic cherry sauce goes very well with a serving of boiled brown rice at about 175kcal per serving.

Ingredients (2 servings):

200g raw frozen prawns

200g chopped tomatoes

25g sachet coconut cream

1 small onion, chopped

1 teaspoon Thai red curry paste

½ teaspoon fresh ginger root

1 teaspoon olive oil

coriander, chopped

Prep time: 5 min

Cooking time: 15 min

Preparation:

Heat the oil in a saucepan. Tip in the onion and ginger and cook for a few minutes until softened. Add the curry paste, stir and cook for 1 more min. Pour over the tomatoes and coconut cream, bring to boil and leave to simmer for 5 min, adding a little boiling water if the concoction gets too thick.

Add the prawns and cook for another 5-10 min. Sprinkle with the chopped coriander and serve.

Nutritional value per serving: 180kcal, 20g protein, 9g fat (4g saturated), 6g carbs (1g fiber, 5g sugar), 1g salt, 18% iron, 10% magnesium, 20% vitamin A, 26% vitamin C, 13% vitamin B3, 25% vitamin B12.

24. Chicken with Mushrooms

A healthy dish, this chicken casserole has a high amount of protein that will keep you full until dinner. The chicken thighs add extra flavor and juiciness, while the mushrooms are responsible for the tangy feel of this low calories midday meal.

Ingredients (2 servings):

250g boneless, skinless chicken thighs

125ml chicken stock

25g frozen peas

150g mushrooms

25g cubetti di pancetta

1 large shallot, chopped

1 tablespoon olive oil

1 teaspoon white wine vinegar

flour, for dusting

small handful parsley, finely chopped

Prep time: 15 min

Cooking time: 25 min

Preparation:

Heat 1 teaspoon of oil in a non-stick frying pan, season and dust the chicken with the flour. Brown on all sides then remove the chicken and fry the pancetta and mushrooms until softened.

And the rest of the olive oil and cook the shallots for 5 min. Add the stock, the vinegar and bubble for 1-2 min. Return the chicken, pancetta and mushrooms to the pan and cook for 15 min. Add the peas and parsley, cook for 2 more minutes, then serve.

Nutritional value per serving: 260kcal, 32g protein, 13g fat (3g saturated), 4g carbs (3g fiber, 1 g sugar), 1g salt, 21% iron, 39% vitamin D, 12% vitamin B2, 34% vitamin B3, 17% vitamin B6.

25. Turkey Stir Fry

High in protein, quickly made and flavorsome, this dish is a perfect, spicy lunch. Its carbs content will load you with energy so it can also be an ideal pre-workout meal.

Ingredients (2 servings):

200g turkey breast steaks, cut into strips (remove fat)

150g rice noodles

170g green beans, halved

1 garlic clove, sliced

1 small red onion, sliced

½ red chili, finely chopped

juice from ½ lime

½ teaspoon olive oil

½ teaspoon chili powder

1 teaspoon fish sauce

Mint, roughly chopped

Coriander, roughly chopped

Prep time: 10 min

Cooking time: 15 min

Preparation:

Cook the noodles following the instructions on the pack. Heat the oil in a non-stick pan and fry the turkey over a high heat for 2 min. Add the onion, garlic and beans and cook for another 5 min.

Tip over the lime juice, fresh chili, chili powder and fish sauce, stir and cook for 3 min. Stir in the noodles and herbs according to taste and serve.

Nutritional value per serving: 425kcal, 32g protein, 3g fat (1g saturated), 71g carbs (4g fiber, 4g sugar), 1 g salt, 12% iron, 10% magnesium, 12% vitamin A, 36% vitamin C, 13% vitamin B1, 24% vitamin B2.

26. Tangy Trout

Try this easy, healthy trout recipe for a light summer meal. A great source of vitamin B12, this lemony white fish can be served with a side of green salad sprinkled with sea salt and a bit of lemon juice for an extra zesty feel.

Ingredients (2 servings):

2 trout fillets

15g pine nuts, toasted and roughly chopped

25g breadcrumbs

1 teaspoon soft butter

1 teaspoon olive oil

juice and zest from ½ lemon

1 small bunch of parsley, chopped

Prep time: 10 min

Cooking time: 5 min

Preparation:

Heat the grill to high. Lay the fillets, skin side down on an oiled baking tray.

Mix the breadcrumbs, lemon juice and zest, butter, parsley and half the pine nuts. Scatter the composition in a thin layer over the fillets, drizzle with the oil and place under the grill for 5 min. Sprinkle over the rest of the pine nuts and serve with steamed cauliflower or green beans.

Nutritional value per serving: 298kcal, 30g protein, 16g fat (4g saturated), 10g carbs (1g fiber, 1g sugar), 11% magnesium, 14% vitamin B1, 41% vitamin B3, 25% vitamin B6, 150% vitamin B12.

27. Spicy Seafood Stew

Treat your senses to this spicy mix of prawns, clams and white fish that delivers a hearty amount of protein and covers most of the B vitamins. Make sure to use fresh seafood to maximize the savory taste of this one-pot casserole.

Ingredients (2 servings):

100g large peeled raw prawns

150g clams

150g white fish fillets (cut into 3 cm pieces)

250g small new potatoes, halved and boiled

130g chopped tomatoes

350ml chicken stock

1 small onion, chopped

2 garlic cloves, chopped

1 dried ancho chili

juice from 1 lime

½ teaspoon smoked hot paprika

½ teaspoon ground cumin

1 teaspoon olive oil

lime wedges for serving (optional)

Prep time: 15 min

Cooking time: 30 min

Preparation:

Toast the chilies in a hot, dry frying pan until they puff up a bit, then remove, deseed and stem them. Soak in boiling water for 15 min.

Heat the olive oil in a large pan, add the onion, garlic and season and cook until softened. Add the paprika, chili, cumin, tomatoes and stock and sauté for 5 min, then puree in a blender until smooth. Pour back into the pan and bring to the boiling point. Let it simmer for 10 min. Add the prawns, fish fillets, clams and potatoes, place a lid on top of the pan and cook for 5 min over a medium-high heat. Serve with lime wedges if you like.

Nutritional value per serving: 347kcal, 44g protein, 6g fat (1 g saturated), 28g carbs (4g fiber, 7g sugar), 1.1g salt, 18% magnesium, 12% vitamin A, 40% vitamin C, 16%

vitamin B1, 10% vitamin B2, 23% vitamin B3, 26% vitamin B6, 62% vitamin B12.

DINNER

28. Stuffed Eggplant

A savory veggie meal, with a crisp cheese and breadcrumbs topping, that is light and perfect for dinner. Forget stuffed peppers and try this flavored eggplant instead.

Ingredients (2 serving):

1 eggplant

60g vegetarian mozzarella, torn into pieces

1 small onion, finely chopped

2 garlic cloves, finely chopped

1 tablespoon olive oil, plus extra for drizzling

2 garlic cloves, finely chopped

6 cherry tomatoes, cut in half

a handful of basil leaves, chopped

a few fresh whole eat breadcrumbs

Prep time: 15 min

Cooking time: 40 min

Preparation:

Heat the oven to 200C fan/gas 7. Slash the eggplant lengthways in half (you can leave the stem intact or remove it). Cut a border inside the eggplant about 1 cm thick. Using a teaspoon, scoop out the eggplant flesh until you are left with 2 shells. Chop the flesh then place it aside. Brush the shells with a little oil, season and place them in a baking dish. Cover it with a foil and bake for 20 min.

Add the remaining oil to a non-stick frying pan. Add the onion and cook until it is soft, then tip in the chopped eggplant flesh and cook through. Add the garlic and tomatoes and cook for another 3 min.

When the eggplant shells are tender, remove them from the oven, stuff them, sprinkle some breadcrumbs and drizzle with a little bit of oil. Reduce the heat in the oven to 180C fan/ gas 6. Bake for 15-20 min, until the cheese has melted and the breadcrumbs are golden. Serve with a green salad.

Nutritional value per serving: 266kcal, 9g protein, 20g fat (6g saturated), 14g carbs (5g fiber, 7g sugar), 1g salt, 15% vitamin A, 19% calcium.

29. Orange, Walnut and Blue Cheese Salad

Try this salty and sweet salad with crumbled blue cheese and chopped walnuts for a light supper. This, high in healthy fats and vitamin C, no cook recipe takes only 10 min to make and is a great way to end a busy day.

Ingredients (2 servings):

1*100g bag of bag of mixed salad (spinach, rocket and watercress)

1 large orange

40g walnuts, roughly chopped

70g blue cheese, crumbled

1 teaspoon walnut oil

Prep time: 10 min

No cooking

Preparation:

Empty the salad bag into a bowl. Peel the oranges and cut the segments from the pith over a small bowl to catch the juice. Whisk the walnut oil into the orange juice then pour over the salad leaves. Toss the salad, scatter over the orange segments, blue cheese and walnuts and serve.

Nutritional value per serving: 356kcal, 14g protein, 30g fat (10g saturated), 8g carbs (3g fiber, 8g sugar), 19% calcium, 10% magnesium, 20% vitamin A, 103% vitamin C, 10% vitamin B1.

30. Mexican Rice and Bean Salad

A low fat spicy meal with Latin American flavors, the Mexican rice and bean salad is packed with vegetables and makes for a filling supper. Tweak it a little and use a can of mixed beans for a more colorful plate.

Ingredients (2 servings):

90g brown rice

200g can black bean salad, drained

½ ripe avocado, chopped

2 spring onions, chopped

½ red pepper, deseeded and chopped

Juice from ½ lime

1 teaspoon Cajun spice mix

small bunch of coriander, chopped

Prep time: 15 min

Cooking time: 20 min

Preparation:

Cook the rice following the instructions on the pack. Drain then cool under running water until cold. Stir in the beans, pepper, onions and avocado.

Mix the lime juice with black pepper and the Cajun spices then pour over the rice. Add the coriander and serve.

Nutritional value per serving: 326kcal, 11g protein, 10g fat (2g saturated), 44g carbs (6g fiber, 4g sugar), 10% iron, 15% magnesium, 11% vitamin B1, 13% vitamin B6.

31. Chickpeas and Spinach Curry

Whip up this warming meal for a great night in. High in vitamin A and protein, this veggie dish can be served with a bit of Naan. Watch out for the extra calories though, one piece of Naan bread contains about 140kcal.

Ingredients (2 servings):

1*400g can chickpeas, drained

200g cherry tomatoes

130g baby spinach leaves

1 tablespoon curry paste

1 small onion, chopped

lemon juice

Prep time: 5 min

Cooking time: 15 min

Preparation:

Heat the curry paste in a non-stick frying pan. When it starts to split, add the onion and cook for 2 min until it softens. Tip in the tomatoes and bubble until the sauce has reduced.

Add the chickpeas and some seasoning and cook for an extra minute. Take off the heat, then tip the spinach (the heat of the pan will wilt the leaves). Season, add the lemon juice and serve.

Nutritional value per serving: 203kcal, 9g protein, 4g fat, 28g carbs (6g fiber, 5g sugar), 1.5g salt, 25% iron, 29% magnesium, 129% vitamin A, 61% vitamin C, 58% vitamin B6.

32. Thai Vegetable and Coconut Milk Broth

A serving of egg noodles topped with a delicious vegetable broth gives you a delectable and quick taste of Thai. If you prefer a thicker broth, use less vegetable stock, according to taste.

Ingredients (2 servings):

200ml can half-fat coconut milk

500ml vegetable stock

90g egg noodles

1 carrot, cut into matchsticks

¼ head Chinese leaf, sliced

75g beansprouts

3 cherry tomatoes, halved

2 small spring onions, halved and sliced lengthways

juice form ½ lime

1 ½ teaspoons Thai red curry paste

1 teaspoon brown sugar

1 teaspoon olive oil

handful coriander, roughly chopped

Prep time: 15 min

Cooking time 10 min

Preparation:

Heat the oil in a wok then add the curry paste and fry for 1 min until fragrant. Add the vegetable stock, brown sugar and coconut milk and simmer for 3 min.

Tip in the noodles, carrots and Chinese leaf and simmer until tender. Add the beansprouts and tomatoes, lime juice to taste and some extra seasoning. Spoon into bowls and sprinkle with coriander and spring onions.

Nutritional value: 338kcal, 10g protein, 14g fat (7g saturated), 46g carbs (5g fiber, 12g sugar), 1.2g salt, 14% iron, 16% magnesium, 10% vitamin B3.

33. Stuffed Zucchinis

A healthy veggie supper, light on the stomach and a delight to bake. The zucchinis are flavored by a mix of pine nuts, sundried tomatoes and fine parmesan cheese. You can brush the zucchinis with a bit of pesto instead of olive oil, before placing them in the oven.

Ingredients (2 servings):

2 zucchinis, halved lengthways

2 teaspoons olive oil

mixed salad, to serve

Stuffing:

25g pine nuts

3 spring onions, finely sliced

1 garlic clove, crushed

3 sundried tomatoes in oil, drained

12g parmesan, finely grated

25g dried white breadcrumbs

1 teaspoon thyme leaf

Prep time: 10 min

Cooking time: 35 min

Preparation:

Heat the oven to 200C fan/gas 7. Place the zucchinis in an ovenproof dish, cut-side up. Brush lightly with 1 teaspoon oil and bake for 20 min.

Mix all the stuffing ingredients together in a bowl and season with black pepper, sprinkle the mix on top of the zucchinis and drizzle with the remaining olive oil. Bake for another 10-15 min, until the zucchinis are softened and the topping is crisp. Serve hot with a mixed salad.

Nutritional value per serving: 244kcal, 10g protein, 17g fat (3 saturated), 14g carbs (3g fiber, 5g sugar), 56% vitamin C, 16% vitamin B2, 21% vitamin B6.

34. Fruit Salad

A vitamin C packed fruit salad sweetened with honey and ready to serve in 10 min. Make this simple fruit salad sing by adding a sprinkle of freshly-cut mint.

Ingredients (1 serving):

1 grapefruit, peel and pith cut away

2 apricots, sliced

2 oranges, peel and pith cut away

1 teaspoon clear honey

Prep time 5 min

No cooking

Preparation:

Put the apricots in a large bowl. Segment the oranges and grapefruits into the bowl to catch the juices. Stir in the honey and serve.

Nutritional value per serving: 166kcal, 4g protein, 36g carbs (8g fiber, 28g sugar), 46% vitamin A, 184% vitamin C, 13% vitamin B1.

35. Devilled Mushrooms

Treat yourself to a spicy, healthy meal, with a side of fresh, crisp salad. Double the serving for a higher fiber and protein content or pair it with a medium slice of baguette at about 150kcal per piece.

Ingredients (2 servings):

8 large flat mushrooms

2 garlic cloves, crushed

2 tablespoon olive oil

2 tablespoons Worcestershire sauce

2 tablespoons wholegrain mustard

1 teaspoon paprika

140g bag mixed salad leaves, with watercress and ruby chard

Prep time: 10 min

Cooking time: 15 min

Preparation:

Heat the oven to 180C fan/ gas 6. Mix together the mustard, oil, garlic and Worcestershire sauce in a large bowl, then season with freshly ground black pepper and salt. Add the mushrooms to the mix and toss well to coat them evenly. Place them stalk–side up in an ovenproof dish, sprinkle them with the paprika and bake for 8-10 min.

Divide the salad leaves between two serving plates with 4 mushrooms on each plate. Spoon over the juices and serve immediately.

Nutritional value per serving: 102kcal, 8g protein, 14g fat (2g saturated), 8g carbs (4g fiber), 1g salt, 20% vitamin B2, 16% vitamin B3.

36. Smoked Trout with Beetroot, Fennel and Apple Salad

A delicate hot-smoked fish complemented by a crisp apple and the colorful beetroot, makes for an exotic salad with a gorgeous flavor combination. Trout is an ideal source of B12 and high quality protein.

Ingredients (2 servings):

140g skinless smoked trout fillet

100g baby beetroot in vinegar, drained and quartered

4 spring onions, sliced

1 green-skinned apple, cored, quartered and sliced

½ small fennel bulb, trimmed and thinly sliced

small bunch dill leaves, finely chopped

2 tablespoons low-fat yogurt

1 teaspoon horseradish sauce

Prep time: 10 min

No cooking

Preparation:

Place the fennel in a serving dish and scatter over the beetroots, spring onions and apple. Cut the trout into chunky pieces and put on top. Sprinkle with half the dill.

Mix the yogurt and horseradish with 1 tablespoon cold water, then add the rest of the dill and stir. Pour half of the dressing over the salad and toss lightly, then spoon over the rest of the dressing and serve.

Nutritional value per serving: 183kcal, 19g protein, 5g fat (1g saturated), 16g carbs (5g fiber, 16g sugar), 1.6g salt, 12% iron, 11% vitamin A, 20% vitamin C, 20% vitamin B1, 17% vitamin B2, 20% vitamin B3, 100% vitamin B12.

37. Roasted Carrots with Pomegranate and Goat Cheese

An all-round full meal when it comes to nutrients, this combination of sweet vegetables and sour juices is a healthy and interesting dinner option. Make sure to keep the pomegranate seeds separate and add them just before serving if you plan on making a big batch.

Ingredients (2 servings):

375g carrots

40g pomegranate seeds

50g goat cheese, crumbled

200g can chickpeas, drained

grated zest and juice from ½ orange

1 tablespoon olive oil

1 teaspoon cumin seeds

small bunch mint, chopped

Prep time: 10 min

Cooking time: 50 min

Preparation:

Heat the oven to 170C fan/gas 5. Put the carrots in a bowl and toss with half the olive oil, the cumin seeds and orange zest and salt. Spread the carrots onto a large baking sheet and roast for 50 min until they get tender and catch some color on the edges.

Stir the chickpeas into the roasted carrots, then tip onto a serving platter. Drizzle with the remaining oil and the orange juice. Add the crumbled goat cheese, scatter with the pomegranate seeds and herbs and serve.

Nutritional value per serving: 285kcal, 12 g protein, 15g fat (6g saturated), 30g carbs (6g fiber, 16g sugar), 15% calcium, 12% iron, 14% magnesium, 610% vitamin A, 28% vitamin C, 12% vitamin B1, 18% vitamin B2, 11% vitamin B3, 37% vitamin B6.

38. Lentil, Carrot and Orange Soup

An interesting soup made with orange juice that will more than cover your daily required amount of vitamin C. Healthy, with flavors that work well together, this recipe is a spicy delight. You can thin it with some water if you find it too thick.

Ingredients (2 servings):

75g red lentils

225g carrots, diced

300ml orange juice

1 onion, chopped

600ml vegetable stock

2 tablespoons low-fat yogurt

1 teaspoon cumin seeds

2 teaspoons coriander seeds

freshly chopped coriander to garnish

Prep time: 15min

Cooking time: 35 min

Preparation:

Crush the seeds in a pestle and mortar, then dry-fry for 2 min until lightly browned. Add the lentils, carrots, onion, orange juice, stock and seasoning and bring to a boil. Cover and simmer for 30 min until the lentils have softened.

Transfer the mix to a food processor and blend until smooth. Return to the pan, reheat at medium heat and stir occasionally. Season to taste then ladle into bowls, swirl the yogurt over, sprinkle with the coriander leaves and serve at once.

Nutritional value per serving: 184kcal, 8g protein, 2g fat, 34g carbs (4g fiber), 1g salt, 340% vitamin A, 134% vitamin C, 16% vitamin B1, 11% vitamin B3, 13% vitamin B6.

39. Veggie Red Curry

It might take almost an hour to make, but this fragrant Thai dish will surely get your taste buds into action. Rich in nutrients, this creamy veggie curry has the makings of a standalone dish, but it can be also served with a side of boiled brown rice at around 175 extra kcal.

Ingredients (2 servings):

70g mushrooms, snapped

70g sugar snap peas

½ zucchini, chopped into chunks

½ eggplant, chopped into chunks

100g firm tofu, chopped into cubes

200ml can reduced-fat coconut milk

1 red chili (½ finely chopped, ½ sliced into rounds)

¼ red pepper, deseeded and chopped into chinks

2 tablespoons soy sauce

Juice from 1 lime

1 tablespoon olive oil

10g basil leaves

½ teaspoon brown sugar

Paste:

3 shallots, roughly chopped

2 small red chilies

½ lemongrass, roughly chopped

1 garlic cloves

stalks from 10g pack coriander

½ red pepper, deseeded and roughly chopped

zest form ½ lime

¼ teaspoon grated ginger root

½ teaspoon ground coriander

½ teaspoon freshly ground pepper

Prep time: 30 min

Cooking time: 20 min.

Preparation:

Marinate the tofu in half the lime juice, 1 tablespoon soy sauce and the chopped chili.

Place the paste ingredients in a food processor.

Heat half the oil in a pan, add 2 tablespoons of paste and fry for 2 min. Stir in the coconut milk with 50ml water, the eggplant, zucchini and pepper. Cook until almost tender.

Drain the tofu, pat it dry then fry it in the remaining oil in a small pan until golden.

Add the mushroom, sugar snaps and most of the basil, then season with the sugar, the rest of the lime juice and soy sauce. Cook until the mushrooms are tender, then add the tofu and heat through. Sprinkle with the basil, scatter the sliced chili and serve.

Nutritional value per serving: 233kcal, 8g protein, 18g fat (10g saturated), 11g carbs (3g fiber, 7g sugar), 3g salt, 13% calcium, 12% iron, 14% magnesium, 11% vitamin A, 65% vitamin C, 15% vitamin B1, 21% vitamin B2, 12% vitamin B3, 22% vitamin B6.

40. Mushroom Pilaf with Lemon

This low-fat mushroom pilaf is your ticket to a lighter alternative to risotto. Throw in a handful of green peas for a more colorful dish, and feel free to replace the chives with spring onions if you like.

Ingredients (2 servings):

100g brown rice

150g mushrooms, sliced

250ml vegetable stock

1 small onion, sliced

1 garlic clove, crushed

3 tablespoons light soft cheese with garlic and herbs

zest and juice from ½ lemon

small bunch of chives, snipped

Prep time: 10 min

Cooking time: 30 min

Preparation:

Place the onion in a non-stick pan, add a few tablespoons of the stock and cook for about 5 min until softened. Add the garlic and mushrooms and cook for 2 more minutes. While mixing, add the rice and lemon zest and juice. Pour in the remaining vegetable stock and seasoning and bring to a boil. Turn down the heat, cover the pan and let it simmer for 30 min until the rice is tender. Stir through half of each of the chives and soft cheese. Divide between 2 plates and serve topped with the remaining soft cheese and chives.

Nutritional value per serving : 249kcal, 12g protein, 4g fat (2g saturated), 44g carbs, 2g fiber, 4g sugar), 11% vitamin A, 23% vitamin B2.

FAT REDUCING JUICE RECIPES

1. Apple Mix Juice

This is a great juice to have before exercise or after dinner, and it is a great way of helping you with your weight loss. And why is that? Apples are low in calories and their fiber helps you feel fuller for a longer time, because it expands the stomach, which means fewer calories in your stomach. Cucumber juice is very rich in water, and you know that water is important for weight loss. In a recent study, adults consuming extra water lost 4 pounds of body weight more than those who did not. Apple: Improves neurological health

- Cucumber: Aids in weight loss and digestion
- Lemon: Helps in reducing pain and inflammation in joints and knees
- Orange: Regulates high blood pressure
- Banana: Plays a role in preserving memory and boosts your mood

Ingredients:

- Apple - 1 medium 162g

- Cucumber - 1 cucumber (301g
- Lemon - 1/2 fruit 25g
- Orange - 1 large 154g
- Banana - 1 medium 150 g

How to prepare:

- **Wash all the ingredients. Peel if necessary.**
- **Juice them all together for a great drink.**

Total amount of calories: 280

Vitamins: Vitamin A 27µg, Vitamin C 101.2mg, Calcium 108mg, Vitamin B-6 0.328mg, Vitamin E 1.54mg, Vitamin K 49.7µg

Minerals: Copper 0.418mg, Magnesium 52mg, Phosphorus 137mg, Selenium 2.1µg, Zinc 1.07mg

2. Fruit Mania Juice

Taste this awesome juice that is not only delightful but is also going to help you lose weight faster and cleanse your body. Ingredients like cayenne pepper may help stoke your metabolic fire. Mango, "the fruit of India", as it is sometimes called, has a wealth of nutrients, and it is a superior source of beta-carotene and vitamin C. That means, the more nutrients you get, the less you have to eat per meal. So make sure to add this juice to your daily meals.

- Apple: Protects the body from free radicals effects
- Cayenne Pepper: Possible anti-cancer agent
- Mango: Improves digestion
- Orange: Alkalizes the body
- Banana: Lowers blood pressure

Ingredients:

- Apple – 1 large 213g
- Cayenne Pepper (spice) - 1 pinch 0.11g
- Mango (peeled) - 1 fruit (without grain) 316g
- Orange (peeled) - 1 large 154g

- Banana (peeled) – 1 medium 150 g

How to prepare:

- **Wash all the ingredients. Peel if necessary.**
- **Juice them all together for a great drink.**

Total calories: 265

Vitamins: Vitamin A 128µg, Vitamin C 122.1mg, Vitamin B-6 0.409mg, Vitamin E 2.38mg, Vitamin K 12.1µg, Calcium 68mg, Iron 0.72mg

Minerals: Copper 0.319mg, Magnesium 41mg, Phosphorus 68mg, Selenium 1.9µg, Zinc 0.31mg

3. Apple Magic Juice

This is another delicious juice that will help you improve your lifestyle, and accelerate the rate at which you lose weight. Carrots fight fat because of their fiber content, more than half is soluble fiber calcium pectate. This helps lower blood-cholesterol levels by eliminating bile acids. In the end, cholesterol will be drawn out of the bloodstream to make more bile acids, and this will lower your cholesterol. It also helps eliminate excess fluids from the body. Enjoy this juice and include it in your daily routine. It will give you positive results.

- Apples : Prevent dementia

- Carrots: Prevent stroke

- Ginger Root: Helps control the heart rate

- Lemon: Prevents growth and multiplication of pathogenic bacteria

- Mango: Helps in diabetes

Ingredients:

- Apples - 1 medium 180g

- Carrots - 2 medium 112g

- Ginger Root - 1/2 thumb 10g

- Lemon (peeled) - 1/2 fruit 25g
- Mango (peeled) – 1/2 fruit 70 g

How to prepare:

- **Wash all the ingredients. Peel if necessary.**
- **Juice them all together for a great drink.**

Total calories: 161

Vitamins: Vitamin A 521µg, Vitamin C 17.9mg, Calcium 30mg, Iron 0.53mg, Vitamin B-6 0.212mg, Vitamin E 1.02mg, Vitamin K 12.9µg

Minerals: Copper 0.114mg, Magnesium 21mg, Phosphorus 54mg, Selenium 0.1µg, Zinc 0.25mg

4. Weight Loss Booster Juice

Here is a simple juice recipe, yet very effective for weight loss. Cabbage is not consumed as much as it should be. It's a great source of vitamin C, and has a high content of fiber. Pears are also a good source of fiber. Studies have shown that if you eat more than three pears a day, you will consume fewer calories and you will lose more weight. They also have a really high level of fructose and glucose; this provides a natural source of energy. Pears contain boron and this helps the body to retain calcium, making you healthier. It's a great recipe for you and your family.

- Apple: Reduces the risk of diabetes
- Cabbage: Helps lowering blood pressure
- Lemon: Helps cure the common cold
- Pears: Prevent cancer

Ingredients:

- Apple- 1 medium 180 g
- Cabbage (red) - 3 leaves 72g
- Lemon (with rind) - 1/2 fruit 27g
- Pears - 2 medium 346g

How to prepare:

- **Wash all the ingredients. Peel if necessary.**
- **Juice them all together for a great drink.**

Total calories: 205

Vitamins: Vitamin A 29µg, Vitamin C 48.1mg, Thiamin 0.059mg, Vitamin B-6 0.213mg, Vitamin E 0.3mg, Vitamin K 33.6µg, Calcium 52mg

Minerals: Copper 0.203mg, Magnesium 27mg, Phosphorus 50mg, Selenium 0.6µg, Zinc 0.3mg

5. Super Spinach Juice

Spinach is a great source of fiber for our digestive system. It is a cleansing agent which removes waste that has accumulated over time in the digestive tracts. Because of its laxative effect on the body, it will also improve the tracts functions.Lemon has always been a great ingredient when trying to lose weight, as well as apples, since they help lower your cholesterol. It's a delicious juice that you can enjoy at any time.

- Celery: It helps you calm down
- Lemon: Aids in the production of digestive juices
- Pears: Help in building up your immune system
- Orange: Regulates High Blood Pressure
- Spinach: Keeps the skin and hair healthy
- Apples: Lower bad cholesterol

Ingredients:

- Celery – 3 stalks, large 206g
- Lemon (peeled) – ½ fruit 25g
- Pear- 1 medium 170g
- Orange (peeled) – 1 large 180g

- Spinach – 4 handful 100g
- Apples – 2 medium 350g

How to prepare:

- **Wash all the ingredients. Peel if necessary.**
- **Juice them all together for a great drink.**

Total calories: 243

Vitamins: Vitamin A 406µg, Vitamin C 107.2mg, Calcium 219mg, Iron 3.16mg, Choline 45.9mg, Vitamin B-6 0.56mg, Vitamin K 413.5µg

Minerals: Copper 0.253mg, Magnesium 114mg, Phosphorus 121mg, Selenium 1.3µg, Zinc 0.67mg

6. Wonderful Fresh Juice

If losing weight is your goal, try this juice recipe. It will push you in the right direction. Beets are a great way to cleanse the blood, and strengthen the gall bladder and liver. Carrots help the liver to cleanse and to release more bile, and at the same time will boost your immune system, giving you a healthy body. They also contain beta-carotene which is known for reducing the risk of several cancers. The nutrients contained in this juice will provide you with a lot of fiber, and can easily replace a meal if necessary, but with the advantage of having fewer calories. This is a delicious recipe you should add in your daily life.

- Beetroot: Detoxification support
- Banana: Reduces risk of leukemia
- Carrots: Improve vision
- Pepper: Migraine headache prevention

Ingredients:

- Beetroot - 1/2 beet 40g
- Banana – 1 medium 150g
- Carrots - 3 large 206g

- Pepper (sweet red) - 1/2 medium 54g

How to prepare:

- **Wash all the ingredients. Peel if necessary.**
- **Juice them all together for a great drink.**

Total calories: 85

Vitamins: Vitamin A 1128µg, Vitamin C 59.5mg, Calcium 51mg, Choline 13.4mg, Folate 61µg, Vitamin B-6 0.319mg, Vitamin E 1.27mg

Minerals: Copper 0.047mg, Magnesium 25mg, Phosphorus 65mg, Selenium 0.3µg, Zinc 0.46mg

7. Fountain of life

Here is a healthy and appetizing juice recipe that will help you in losing weight. Beets are very useful in helping the liver to cleanse, that means the liver will help metabolize fat more effectively. The liver will get an additional boost from carrots, as they have powerful properties which will detoxify it. They also eliminate excess fluids that lay in the body. Oranges have about 59 calories per fruit; they are fat-free, and high in fiber. They really help to drop those extra pounds. Only good results can come from drinking this juice.

- Apple: Powerful natural antioxidant
- Beetroot: Fights inflammation
- Carrots: Reduce risk of lung cancer
- Parsley: Excellent blood purifier
- Orange: Provides smart carbs

Ingredients:

- Apple - 1 medium 180g
- Beetroot - 1/2 beet 40g
- Carrots - 3 medium 170g
- Parsley - 1 handful 40g

- Orange (peeled) - 1 medium 140 g

How to prepare:

- **Wash all the ingredients. Peel if necessary.**
- **Juice them all together for a great drink.**

Total calories: 110

Vitamins: Vitamin A 1012µg, Vitamin C 34.8mg, Calcium 109mg, Iron 2.38mg, Vitamin B-6 0.14mg, Vitamin E 1.24mg, Vitamin K 305.2µg

Minerals: Copper 0.127mg, Magnesium 32mg, Phosphorus 88mg, Selenium 0.4µg, Zinc 0.67m

8. Banana Max Juice

Let's see if this delicious juice fits your needs. The great thing about juices is they give you all the nutrients you need. The idea is you eat less and have fewer junk food craving. Celery has high calcium content, and helps controlling high blood pressure. Let's not forget that ginger helps digesting fatty foods, and adding lemon juice to any beverage will help accelerate weight loss. Enjoy this juice whenever you want. It can easily replace any snack.

- Banana: Supports heart health
- Cabbage: High in sulfur, the beautifying mineral
- Celery: Contains good salts
- Cider Vinegar: Kills pathogens, including bacteria
- Ginger root: Controls blood pressure
- Grapes: Reduce risk of cancer

Ingredients:

- Banana (peeled) – 1 medium 150g
- Cabbage (red) – ¼ head, medium 201 g
- Celery – 2stalks, 142g

- Cider Vinegar (apple) – 1 tbsp 14.9g

- Ginger Root – 1 thumb 24g

- Grapes – 14 grapes 80g

How to prepare:

- **Wash all the ingredients. Peel if necessary.**

- **Juice them all together for a great drink.**

Total calories: 130

Vitamins: Vitamin A 108µg, Vitamin C 98mg, Vitamin B-6 0.429mg, Vitamin E 0.64mg, Vitamin K 74.3µg, Niacin 1.202mg, Calcium 142mg

Minerals: Copper 0.211mg, Magnesium 54mg, Phosphorus 107mg, Selenium 1.2µg, Zinc 0.4mg

9. Cooler Juice

Our modern lifestyle makes us take the wrong decisions many times when it comes to diet. Here is a juice recipe that takes just a few minutes to prepare, and it will give you a healthy start to your day. Peaches are low on calories, so they can help you stick to a reduced calorie diet. Basil seeds are a great source of fiber, and they have a reputation for their weight loss benefits. Basil: Reduces inflammation and swelling

- Carrots: Are a powerful antiseptic
- Peaches: Lower risk of cancer
- Apple: Protects neuron cells against oxidative stress

Ingredients:

- Basil (fresh) - 3 leaves 1.5g
- Carrots - 14 medium 854g
- Peaches - 5 medium 750g
- Apple -1 medium 180 g

How to prepare:

- **Wash all the ingredients. Peel if necessary.**

- **Juice them all together for a great drink.**

Total calories: 352

Vitamins: Vitamin A 4079µg, Vitamin C 75mg, Calcium 208mg, Vitamin B-6 0.911mg, Vitamin E 5.83mg, Vitamin K 76.9µg, Choline 56.2mg

Minerals: Copper 0.621mg, Magnesium 102mg, Phosphorus 290mg, Selenium 1.1µg, Zinc 2.25mg

10. Fruit Express Juice

This is a great juice that will help you drop pounds or kilos and increase your energy. The ingredients used in this recipe will help you with your digestion, stimulating the digestive juices, and will lower your cholesterol. If you consume two apples per day, it lowers your cholesterol by as much as 17 percent, so that says a lot. Let's not forget to mention that it's full of nutrients, and the calories consumed are quite low. So you get the same result as a meal, but actually you consume fewer calories. It's definitely ideal for weight loss.

- Apples: Reduce risk of thrombotic stroke
- Carrots: Cleanse the body
- Lemon: Strengthens the liver
- Peaches: Support hearth health
- Banana: Lower blood pressure

Ingredients:

- Apples - 1 large 200g
- Carrots – 8 medium 500g
- Lemon (outer skin cut off) - 1/2 fruit 40g
- Peaches - 2 large 300g

- Banana (peeled) - 1 medium 150g

How to prepare:

- **Wash all the ingredients. Peel if necessary.**
- **Juice them all together for a great drink.**

Total calories: 410

Vitamins: Vitamin A 3128µg, Vitamin C 109.8mg, Calcium 194mg, Vitamin B-6 0.819mg, Vitamin E 4.44mg, Vitamin K 54.3µg, Choline 55.7mg

Minerals: Copper 0.412mg, Magnesium 94mg, Phosphorus 206mg, Selenium 1.2µg, Zinc 1.37mg

11. Gold Juice

This is the perfect juice for you if you are looking for something to help you have a smaller waist line. One of the benefits of using kale is that it provides a large nutritional punch with fewer calorie counts per cup. Celery helps to calm nervousness because it has high calcium content and will help in controlling blood pressure. It also lowers cholesterol levels because of the pectin that can be found in apples, so this juice can turn into a real friend while losing weight.

- Apple: Reduces the risk of developing cancer, diabetes, and heart disease.

- Celery: Delivers up to 10 percent of your daily need for Vitamin A

- Cucumber: Helps prevent diabetes, reduces cholesterol, and controls blood pressure.

- Ginger root: Very effective in alleviating symptoms of gastrointestinal distress

- Kale: Is a great anti-inflammatory food

- Lemon: Helps maintain your immune system

Ingredients:

- Apples - 2 medium   364g

- Celery - 2 stalks, 128g

- Cucumber - 1 cucumber 290g

- Ginger Root - 1 thumb 20g

- Kale - 4 leaves (8-12") 120g

- Lemon - 1/2 fruit 40g

How to prepare:

- **Wash all the ingredients. Peel if necessary.**

- **Juice them all together for a great drink.**

Total calories: 215

Vitamins: Vitamin B-6 0.77mg, Vitamin E 1.09mg, Niacin 2.637mg, Thiamin 0.315mg, Vitamin K 1128.7µg

Minerals: Copper 2.47mg, Magnesium 119mg, Phosphorus 207mg, Zinc 1.65mg

12. Energizer Juice

If you were looking for a juice that will help you with your diet or weight loss, you should consider this one. Beets are a great way for purifying not only the blood, but also your liver, and that is a great thing because it helps metabolize fat, so you get rid of it faster. Carrots help you to eliminate excess fluids from the body, so water retention is reduced, especially for women. You will get an energy boost because of the high content in fiber, and it will be a healthy way to fuel your body.

- Beetroot: great to boost your stamina
- Cabbage: Full of vitamin K, helps with mental function and concentration
- Carrots: Prevent heart disease
- Lemon: Plays the role of blood purifier
- Orange: Protects skin
- Pineapple: Prevents asthma
- Spinach: One of the best sources of dietary potassium

Ingredients:

- Beetroot - 1 beet 155g
- Cabbage (red) - 2 leaves 40g

- Carrots - 2 medium 143g

- Lemon - 1/2 fruit 40g

- Orange - 1 fruit 121g

- Pineapple - 1/3 fruit 206g

- Spinach - 2 handful 50g

How to prepare:

- **Wash all the ingredients. Peel if necessary.**

- **Juice them all together for a great drink.**

Total calories: 195

Vitamins: Vitamin B-6 0.60mg, Vitamin E 1.58mg, Vitamin K 149.6µg, Choline 43.8mg, Folate 261µg, Niacin 2.136mg

Minerals: Copper 0.317mg, Magnesium 97mg, Phosphorus 131mg, Selenium 2.1µg, Zinc 1.22mg

13. Refresh Juice

Beets help detoxify the body, so this juice is perfect for a weight loss program. Drinking lemon juice helps in relaxing the mind and body by reducing stress. Carrots do an awesome job in increasing the production of your white blood cells, and that helps you build a stronger immune system, which leads in the end to a stronger body.

- Apples: Are extremely rich in important antioxidants
- Beetroot: Has anti –cancer effects
- Carrots: High level of beta-carotene acts as an antioxidant to prevent cell damage
- Lemon: Aids the production of digestive juices
- Orange: Fights against viral infections

Ingredients:

- Apple – 1 medium 152g
- Beetroot – 1 beet 165g
- Carrots – 10 medium 560g
- Lemon – ½ fruit 40g
- Oranges (peeled) – 2 fruits 242g

How to prepare:

- **Wash all the ingredients. Peel if necessary.**
- **Juice them all together for a great drink.**

Total calories: 275

Vitamins: Vitamin B-6 0.945mg, Vitamin E 4.01mg, Vitamin K 60.8µg, Choline 71.4mg, Folate 233µg, Niacin 5.101mg

Minerals: Copper 0.40mg, Magnesium 107mg, Phosphorus 243mg, Selenium 2.3µg, Zinc 1.81mg

14. Lemon Taste Juice

Adding lemon juice to a beverage will help increase weight loss. This juice recipe is great for a weight loss diet. Lemons help controlling high blood pressure and are also a great source of Vitamin C. It is best served after dinner and combined with an active lifestyle. All of these ingredients will help you lower your cholesterol, and will resolve all your indigestion problems.

- Blueberry: Neutralizes free radicals which might cause disease and aging

- Lemon: Helps balancing the calcium and oxygen levels in the liver

- Pomegranate: Regenerates cell

Ingredients:

- Blueberry - 1 cup 128g

- Lemon - 1/4 fruit 20g

- Pomegranate - 1 pomegranate (262g

How to prepare;

- **Wash all the ingredients.**

- **The pomegranate can be added with the membrane attached, you save some time, and the taste will still be great.**
- **Juice them all together for a great drink.**

Total calories: 168

Vitamins: Vitamin A 3μg, Vitamin C 27mg, Vitamin B-6 0.209mg, Vitamin E 1.6mg, Vitamin K 49.4μg, Choline 21mg, Folate 63μg

Minerals: Copper 0.346mg, Magnesium 28mg, Phosphorus 76mg, Selenium 1.2μg, Zinc 0.57mg

15. Feel Alive Juice

This is a wonderful juice for those of you who like peppermint. Ginger plays a big role in lowering LDL cholesterol, because the spice in it reduces the entire amount of cholesterol that gets absorbed. It also helps with the digestion of fatty foods and breaking down proteins. Oranges have an alkaline effect in the digestive system that stimulates digestive juices, so you get a more active metabolism. Give it a try. It will help you get rid of those hard to lose kilograms or pounds.

- Fennel Bulb: Has good levels of heart-friendly electrolyte potassium
- Ginger Root: Contains health benefiting essential oils
- Lemon: It balances and maintains the pH levels in the body
- Orange: Reduces risk of liver cancer
- Peppermint: Inhibits growth of prostate cancer

Ingredients:

- Fennel Bulb (whole with fronds) - 1 bulb 200g
- Ginger Root - 1/2 thumb 14g
- Lemon - 1/2 fruit 25g

- Orange (peeled) - 1 large 160g
- Peppermint - 5 leaves 0.25g

How to prepare:

- **Wash all the ingredients. Peel if necessary.**
- **Juice them all together for a great drink.**

Total calories: 84

Vitamins: Vitamin A 14µg, Vitamin C 79.4mg, Vitamin B-6 0.144mg, Folate 66µg, Niacin 1.358mg, Riboflavin 0.101mg

Minerals: Copper 0.173mg, Magnesium 36mg, Phosphorus 96mg, Selenium 2mg, Zinc 0.41mg

16. Apple Heart Juice

This juice will help you get healthier and lose weight at the same time. Nutrients from juices are easily absorbed by our bodies and that will equate to a faster metabolism. Apples help you lower your cholesterol because of the pectin they contain. Lemons are always great when trying to drop the fat in your body. Just think of this juice as a friend who wants to help you lose some weight.

- Apple: Prevents breast cancer
- Cranberries: Reduce risk of cardiovascular disease
- Ginger Root: Has anti-inflammatory effects
- Lemon: Prevents formation of wrinkles and acne

Ingredients:

- Apples - 3 medium 500g
- Cranberries - 1/2 cup 50g
- Ginger Root - 1/4 thumb 6g
- Lemon - 1/2 fruit 42g

How to prepare:

- **Wash all the ingredients. Peel if necessary.**
- **Juice them all together for a great drink.**

Total calories: 204

Vitamins: Vitamin A 23µg, Vitamin C 101.5mg, Iron 0.68mg, Vitamin B-6 0.214mg, Vitamin E 1.19mg, Vitamin K 9.2µg, Calcium 76mg

Minerals: Copper 0.193mg, Magnesium 35mg, Phosphorus 61mg, Selenium 0.7µg, Zinc 0.25mg

17. Any Time Juice

Losing fat comes as a result of drinking natural juices, and here is one recipe you will really like. Ginger's greatest benefit is that it will help you digest fatty foods and break down proteins. Spinach has high fiber content, so that helps you get more energy for lower calories. Celery is considered by many a negative-calorie food and by adding celery to your diet, you will increase your weight loss results without so much effort. Taste it, feel it, and let it help you with your daily weight loss routine.

- Apples: Reduce risk of stroke
- Celery: Aids digestion
- Cucumber: Relieves bad breath
- Ginger root: Has anti-microbial effects
- Lemon: Maintains the health of the eyes
- Lime: Excellent weight reducer
- Spinach: Cancer prevention

Ingredients:

- Apples - 2 medium 350g
- Celery - 3 stalks, large 182g

- Cucumber - 1 cucumber 300g

- Ginger Root - 1/2 thumb 10g

- Lemon (with rind) - 1/2 fruit 41g

- Lime (with rind) - 1 fruit 65g

- Spinach - 2 cups 50g

How to prepare:

- **Wash all the ingredients. Peel if necessary.**

- **Juice them all together for a great drink.**

Total calories: 185

Vitamins: Vitamin A 648µg, Vitamin C 198.9mg, Calcium 304mg, Vitamin B-6 0.422mg, Vitamin E 2.39mg, Vitamin K 1904.6µg, Niacin 2.607mg

Minerals: Copper 0.395mg, Magnesium 129mg, Phosphorus 201mg, Selenium 1.9µg, Zinc 2.04mg

18. Lemony Apple Juice

Drinking juice is a great way to get concentrated nutrients into our body. This next recipe is a great one, it helps our digestive system function better by cleansing the stomach and kidneys, and that leads ultimately to a stronger body. This juice will lower your cholesterol because of the particular ingredients it has. Watermelon juice prevents the clogging of arteries and at the same time increases the HDL, which is the good cholesterol. This is a great juice to have before any exercise routine, it is an excellent source of energy.

- Lemon: Aids in production of digestive juices
- Tomato: Maintains blood pressure
- Watermelon: Prevents asthma
- Apple: Improves neurological health

Ingredients:

- Lemon - 1/2 fruit 40g
- Tomato - 1 large whole 171g
- Watermelon - 1 large wedge 560g
- Apple – 1 medium 175g

How to prepare:

- **Wash all the ingredients. Peel if necessary.**

- **Juice them all together for a great drink.**

Total calories: 135

Vitamins: Vitamin A 176μg, Vitamin C 68.5mg, Vitamin B-6 0.326mg, Vitamin E 0.98mg, Vitamin K 11.5μg, Calcium 58mg, Iron 1.70mg

Minerals: Copper 0.264mg, Magnesium 57mg, Phosphorus 69mg, Selenium 1.6μg, Zinc 0.61mg

19. Green Power Juice

Juices are a great way of keeping our body healthy and help us get in shape. Every time you mash up foods like vegetables or fruits, they become incredibly easier to absorb. It means all the vital nutrients will be absorbed into the body at a faster rate than vitamins or other supplements. Carrots eliminate excess fluids from the body, and because of vitamin A and Beta-carotene, carrots may reduce the risk of several cancers. It's a great way to protect and nourish your body with just one drink.

- Apple: Lowers levels of bad cholesterol
- Cabbage: Helps detoxify the body
- Carrots: Prevent heart disease
- Ginger Root: Contains health benefiting essential oils
- Spinach: Contributes to bone health

Ingredients:

- Apples - 2 medium 364g
- Cabbage (red) - 1/4 head, 140g
- Carrots - 4 medium 244g
- Ginger Root - 1/2 10g

- Spinach - 4 handful 100g

How to prepare:

- **Wash all the ingredients. Peel if necessary.**
- **Juice them all together for a great drink.**

Total calories: 200

Vitamins: Vitamin A 1818µg, Vitamin C 120mg, Vitamin B-6 0.73mg, Vitamin E 3.2mg, Vitamin K 404.1µg, Calcium 198mg, Niacin 2.936mg

Minerals: Copper 0.288mg, Magnesium 111mg, Phosphorus 161mg, Selenium 1.7µg, Zinc 1.15mg

20. Morning Start

People are in serious need of a healthy alternative to eating artificial and processed foods. Too many people gain weight because they can't control how much they eat. Certain protein compounds in spinach are beneficial in lowering high blood pressure. The pectin in apples, pears and carrots lowers cholesterol levels as well. Ginger increases blood circulation, and because of this great mixture, you get a high amount of fructose and glucose, making sure you have the necessary energy for an active day. This juice can be enjoyed in the morning or after dinner; it is a super drink when trying to eat higher quality food contents.

- Apple: Reduces the risk of diabetes
- Carrots: Maintain a healthy glowing skin
- Cucumber: Reduces cholesterol and controls blood pressure
- Ginger Root: Helps improve the intestinal motility
- Pear: Beneficial for your colon health
- Spinach: Prevents constipation and promote a healthy digestive tract

Ingredients:

- Apple - 1 medium 180g
- Carrots - 5 medium 300g
- Cucumber - 1 cucumber 300g
- Ginger Root - 1 thumb 24g
- Pear - 1 medium 165g
- Spinach - 2 handful 50g

How to prepare:

- **Wash all the ingredients. Peel if necessary.**
- **Juice them all together for a great drink.**

Total calories: 211

Vitamins: Vitamin A 1863µg, Vitamin C 60.9mg, Vitamin B-6 0.545mg, Vitamin E 2.37mg, Vitamin K 220.1µg, Calcium 151mg, Iron 2.8mg

Minerals: Copper 0.408mg, Magnesium 104mg, Phosphorus 164mg, Selenium 1.2µg, Zinc 1.28mg

21. Simply Celery

Juicing is really the art of extracting the liquid and nutrients from any fruit or vegetable. It helps create energy and vitality like few pills can achieve. This recipe will improve the rate at which you lose weight, and at the same time give you all the daily vitamins and minerals your body needs. The human body is about 75% water, so for proper bodily function, digestion and detoxification, the recommended daily intake is around 2.5 liters. Water is a strong element when trying to drop weight, so you have to concentrate on drinking a lot of it. By having this juice, you get a concentrated portion of the daily liquid requirements that your body needs, with nutrients and fiber that will provide you with a high boost of energy throughout the day.

- Apples: Reduce risk of diabetes
- Celery: Reduces inflammation
- Tangerine: Heals cuts, wounds

Ingredients:

- Apples - 2 large 440g
- Celery - 8 stalks, large 510g
- Tangerine (peeled) - 1 small 76g

How to prepare:

- **Wash all the ingredients. Peel if necessary.**
- **Juice them all together for a great drink.**

Total calories: 180

Vitamins: Vitamin A 101µg, Vitamin C 57.2mg, Calcium 162mg, Vitamin B-6 0.427mg, Vitamin E 1.5mg, Vitamin K 101.7µg, Choline 30mg

Minerals: Copper 0.217mg, Magnesium 61mg, Phosphorus 127mg, Selenium 1.3µg, Zinc 0.45mg

22. Full of Energy

This juice has a high concentration of potassium and phosphorous, which are necessary for normal body function. Tomato juice serves as a great antioxidant and will also improve digestive function. The high content of vitamin C in this juice will help in maintaining the structural integrity of bones. Onion is great to use in any recipe, because it has a low-calorie/high fiber ratio which is exactly what you need when reducing fat in the body.

- Cucumber: Fights cancers
- Onion : Scavenges free radicals
- Parsley : Great immunity booster
- Pepper : Helps relieve allergies
- Tomatoes: Reduces risk of prostate cancer

Ingredients:

- Cucumber - 1 cucumber 300g
- Onion (spring/scallion) - 1 medium 15g
- Parsley - 1 handful 40g
- Pepper (sweet red) - 1/2 medium 55g
- Tomatoes - 2 small whole 180g

How to prepare:

- **Wash all the ingredients. Peel if necessary.**
- **Juice them all together for a great drink.**

Total calories: 68

Vitamins: Vitamin A 260μg, Vitamin C 126mg, Calcium 102mg, Vitamin B-6 0.412mg, Vitamin E 2.06mg, Vitamin K 522.6μg, Calcium 90mg

Minerals: Copper 0.252mg, Magnesium 71mg, Phosphorus 114mg, Selenium 0.7μg, Zinc 1.12mg

23. Sweet Carrots

"Sweet Carrots" will help you keep your body healthy and lose weight at the same time. Bell pepper juice will significantly help in reducing cholesterol. Carrots contain beta-carotene which helps reduce the risk of cancer. The high quantity of vitamins and minerals found in this juice will definitely accelerate the rate at which you get rid of fat and start looking slimmer.

- Carrots: Replenish daily vitamins
- Celery: Aids digestion
- Cucumber: Great source of B vitamins
- Parsley: Great blood builder
- Pepper: Helps produce saliva due to cayenne
- Tomatoes: The folic acid in tomatoes can help with depression

Ingredients:

- Carrots - 2 large 144g
- Celery - 3 stalks, large 192g
- Cucumber - 1/2 cucumber 150.5g
- Parsley - 2 handful 80g

- Pepper (sweet green) - 1/2 medium 58g
- Tomatoes - 3 medium whole 360g

How to prepare:

- **Wash all the ingredients. Peel if necessary.**
- **Juice them all together for a great drink.**

Total calories: 107

Vitamins: Vitamin A 1227µg, Vitamin C 142.3mg, Vitamin B-6 0.642mg, Vitamin E 3.15mg, Vitamin K 1013.3µg, Calcium 212mg, Iron 5.55mg

Minerals: Copper 0.416mg, Magnesium 105mg, Phosphorus 200mg, Selenium 1.1µg, Zinc 1.80mg

24. Lime Delight

"Lime Delight" combines healthy natural fruits and vegetables into a single drink that will make you feel full of energy and ready for a new day. Pectin found in apples can lower your cholesterol by as much as 15 percent. Also, bell peppers help your body to increase your metabolism by lowering triglycerides, which will really make a difference when losing weight. You should consume this juice to start your day and feel the difference by the end of it.

- Apples: Help in losing weight
- Cilantro: Very rich in numerous anti- oxidants
- Cucumbers: Relieve you from bad breath
- Lime: Helps flush out toxins
- Pepper: Remedy for toothache

Ingredients:

- Apples - 2 medium 360g
- Cilantro - 1 bunch 90g
- Cucumbers - 2 cucumbers 600g
- Lime (with rind) - 1/2 fruit 30g

- Pepper (sweet green) (seeds removed) - 1/2 medium 56g

How to prepare:

- **Wash all the ingredients. Peel if necessary.**
- **Juice them all together for a great drink.**

Total calories: 179

Vitamins: Vitamin A 244µg, Vitamin C 79.2mg, Vitamin B-6 0.442mg, Vitamin E 2.1mg, Vitamin K 227.6µg, Calcium 128mg, Iron 2.68mg

Minerals: Copper 0.419mg, Magnesium 80mg, Phosphorus 153mg, Selenium 1.8µg, Zinc 1.25mg

25. Colorful Juice

I think weight loss can be a challenge for anyone who can't control how and what they eat, but with persistence and a serious mindset you can achieve anything. "Colorful Juice" will help you get closer to your goal. Asparagus contains 3 grams of fiber that will quickly cleanse the digestive system. As for celery, it helps to calm the craving for sweets, and helps in controlling high blood pressure. It contains probiotics that selectively stimulate the growth of friendly bacteria in the gut, which will aid digestion. Let's not forget to mention the high amount of nutrients that will get absorbed easier as well. This is a must drink juice if you are serious about getting in shape.

- Asparagus: Great source of nutrients
- Carrots: Vitamin A assists the liver in flushing out the toxins from the body
- Celery: Very low in calories, great choice for losing weight
- Apple: Regulates blood sugar

Ingredients:

- Asparagus - 4 spears, medium 60g

- Carrots - 3 large 216g
- Celery - 2 stalks, large 128g
- Apple – 1 medium 180g

How to prepare:

- **Wash all the ingredients. Peel if necessary.**
- **Juice them all together for a great drink.**

Total calories: 71

Vitamins: Vitamin A 1259μg, Vitamin C 14.1mg, Calcium 87mg, Iron 1.40mg, Vitamin B-6 0.302mg, Vitamin E 1.55mg, Vitamin K 61.5μg

Minerals: Copper 0.173mg, Magnesium 31mg, Phosphorus 81mg, Selenium 1.3μg, Zinc 0.61mg

26. Holiday Juice

Juicing is a fun and easy way to get fruits and veggies into your diet. This recipe is both healthy and delicious. One great benefit of adding kale into your juice is that it provides a large nutritional punch with one of the fewest calorie counts per cup in all vegetables, and that means it will help you look slimmer faster. Lemon juice helps in lowering cholesterol and gets rid of fat. You should serve this juice 30 minutes before any meal to get the most from it.

- Apples: Contain pectin and lower the LDL (bad cholesterol)
- Celery: Helps in controlling high blood pressure
- Cucumber: Contains silica, essential component of healthy connective tissue
- Ginger root: Ameliorates effects on digestive aliments
- Kale: Helps support a healthy immune system
- Lemon: Assists in curing respiratory problems
- Orange: Helps stimulate white cells to fight infection

Ingredients:

- Apples - 3 medium 540g

- Celery - 3 stalks, large 190g

- Cucumber - 1/2 cucumber 150.5g

- Ginger Root - 1/2 thumb 10g

- Kale - 4 leaves 140g

- Lemon - 1 fruit 50g

- Orange (peeled, de-seeded) - 1 large 180g

How to prepare:

- **Wash all the ingredients. Peel if necessary.**

- **Juice them all together for a great drink.**

Total calories: 295

Vitamins: Vitamin A 531µg, Vitamin C 212.8mg, Calcium 294mg, Iron 2.69mg, Vitamin B-6 0.627mg, Vitamin E 1.3mg, Vitamin K 735.8µg

Minerals: Copper 1.664mg, Magnesium 103mg, Phosphorus 211mg, Selenium 2.4µg, Zinc 1.19mg

27. Spinach Power

"Spinach Power" can replace a snack or even part of your breakfast, in the morning, if you are really hungry. It's a great source of energy and nutrients. To have a stronger body, you need all body functions to work efficiently. Beets have shown to help cleanse the blood, and help metabolize fat. Let's not forget that they are high in carbohydrates so they are a great source of energy. Celery is a great source of vitamin C and is high in fiber, which is important for the body.

- Apples: They lower risk of developing lung cancer
- Beetroot: Is a great treatment used for leukemia
- Carrots: Beta- carotene consumption reduces risk of several cancers
- Spinach: Slows down cancerous cell division, in breast cancer

Ingredients:

- Apple - 1 medium 180g
- Beetroot - 1 beet 175g
- Carrots - 8 medium 480g
- Spinach - 3 cups 90g

How to prepare:

- **Wash all the ingredients. Peel if necessary.**
- **Juice them all together for a great drink.**

Total calories: 190

Vitamins: Vitamin A 3074µg, Vitamin C 50.5mg, Calcium 218mg, Vitamin B-6 0.765mg, Vitamin E 3.05mg, Vitamin K 368.6µg, Iron 4.01mg

Minerals: Copper 0.373mg, Magnesium 125mg, Phosphorus 215mg, Selenium 2.1µg, Zinc 1.35mg

28. Health Supplier

To live better and feel great you need to stay away from junk food. This juice will supply the body with a lot of the nutrients it requires. Make this juice in the morning as a great source of energy, and it will help maintain your metabolism active for the entire day. Choline contained by beets juice is a great way to detoxify the entire digestive system. A carrot a day reduces stroke risk by 68 percent so you may think twice before skipping your vegetables. High amounts of nutrients make this juice a great way to fuel your body for the entire day accompanied by healthy food.

- Apples: May protect brain cells from the free radical damage that leads to Alzheimer.

- Beetroot: Unique source of betaine, a nutrient that helps protecting cells

- Carrots: The high level of beta-carotene acts as an antioxidant to cell damage

- Celery: It regulates the body's alkaline balance

- Ginger Root: Helps with arthritis-related problems

- Cucumber: Rehydrates the body and replenishes vitamins

Ingredients:

- Apples - 2 medium 360g
- Beetroot - 1 beet 175g
- Carrots - 4 medium 240g
- Celery - 3 stalks, 192g
- Ginger Root - 1/2 thumb 10g
- Cucumber - 1/2 cucumber 150g

How to prepare:

- **Wash all the ingredients. Peel if necessary.**
- **Juice them all together for a great drink.**

Total calories: 215

Vitamins: Vitamin A 1370μg, Vitamin C 34.2mg, Vitamin B-6 0.557mg, Vitamin E 2.04mg, Vitamin K 83.1μg, Calcium 160mg, Iron 2.40mg

Minerals: Copper 0.327mg, Magnesium 84mg, Phosphorus 167mg, Selenium 1.6μg, Zinc 1.25mg

29. Good Life

"Good Life" is vital to maintain good health and can improve your weight loss. It's easy to prepare and you get the maximum benefits when all the ingredients are fresh. Beets are great fuel for our body, containing high amounts of fiber essential to the body. Spirulina contains all the essential amino acids the body needs which will definitely be a great source when trying to get slimmer.

- Beetroot: Useful in helping cleanse the liver
- Celery: Protects the eyes and prevents age-related degeneration of vision
- Spinach: High level of iron makes it a great blood builder
- Spirulina: Increases stamina and immunity

Ingredients:

- Beetroot - 1 beet 175g
- Celery - 2 stalks, large 128g
- Spinach - 3 cups 90g
- Spirulina (dried) - 1 teaspoon 2.31g

How to prepare:

- Wash all the ingredients. Peel if necessary.
- Juice them all together for a great drink.

Total calories: 52

Vitamins: Vitamin A 308μg, Vitamin C 23.7mg, Vitamin B-6 0.257mg, Vitamin E 1.45mg, Vitamin K 311.1μg, Calcium 110mg, Iron 3.12mg

Minerals: Copper 0.291mg, Magnesium 90mg, Phosphorus 100mg, Selenium 2μg, Zinc 0.78m

30. Roll the Beet

Juices have been around for a long time and are one of the best ways to absorb all the nutrients that fruits and vegetables have to offer. "Roll the Beet" is simple to prepare and due to the low calorie intake, you will see great results soon after drinking it. The best time of the day to drink it is in the morning so you can start the day with a big boost of energy to keep you active.

- Beetroot: Lowers blood pressure in a short period of time
- Carrots: Great source of beta-carotene
- Oranges: Fight against Viral infections

Ingredients:

- Beetroot - 1 beet 170g
- Carrots - 2 medium 120g
- Oranges - 2 fruits 262g

How to prepare:

- **Wash all the ingredients. Peel if necessary.**
- **Juice them all together for a great drink.**

Total calories: 115

Vitamins: Vitamin A 726µg, Vitamin C 104.6mg, Vitamin B-6 0.29mg, Vitamin E 0.84mg, Vitamin K 11.1µg, Calcium 111mg, Iron 1.40mg

Minerals: Copper 0.211mg, Magnesium 55mg, Phosphorus 102mg, Selenium 1.7µg, Zinc 0.73mg

31. Life Punch

When you are in a rush, it's easy to be tempted to go for canned or processed foods that are out in the market simply because they are easy to attain. But easier isn't always the best way on the long term. The easy way of having a healthy daily snack that provides you with all the vitamins is juicing, and this juice is packed with vital ingredients that will improve your immune system and will fill your body with what it needs to function properly and efficiently.

- Beetroot : Prevents cancer
- Carrots : Great way of protecting the skin from the sun
- Celery : Aids digestion, increases weight loss
- Ginger Root: Has anti-inflammatory effects
- Lime : It balances and maintains the pH level of the body
- Pepper: Supports Weight loss
- Spinach : Maintains muscle and nerve function

Ingredients:

- Beetroot - 170g
- Carrots - 210g

- Celery - 2 stalks, 125g
- Ginger Root - 1 thumb 20g
- Lime - 1/2 fruit 30g
- Pepper (jalapeno) - 1 pepper 10g
- Spinach - 2 cups 60g

How to prepare:

- **Wash all the ingredients. Peel if necessary.**
- **Juice them all together for a great drink.**

Total calories: 107

Vitamins: Vitamin A 1457µg, Vitamin C 48.4mg, Vitamin B-6 0.507mg, Vitamin E 2.49mg, Vitamin K 241.1µg, Calcium 155mg, Iron 3.01mg

Minerals: Copper 0.301mg, Magnesium 96mg, Phosphorus 151mg, Selenium 2µg, Zinc 1.21mg

32. Weight Fighter

"Weight Fighter" will make a difference for sure in your fight to get rid of fat, if it's consumed just a few times per week. These fruits and vegetables have a lot to offer because of the greens and roots it has. Beet greens are the leaves that come with the beet, they have a high concentration of vitamins when washed and blended into your juice.

- Apple: Because of the pectin, helps lose weight

- Beet Greens: They boost your stamina and fight inflammation

- Beetroot: Has anti-cancer effects

- Carrots: Improve vision and have an anti-aging effect

- Celery: Aids digestion because of the high water content combined with insoluble fiber

- Ginger root: Has a painkiller effect

Ingredients:

- Apple - 1 large 220g

- Beet Greens (optional) - 3 leaves 95g

- Beetroot - 1 beet 175g

- Carrots - 4 medium 240g

- Celery - 1 stalk, large 60g

- Ginger Root - 1/2 thumb 10g

How to prepare:

- **Wash all the ingredients. Peel if necessary.**

- **Juice them all together for a great drink.**

Total calories: 157

Vitamins: Vitamin A 1645µg, Vitamin C 45.1mg, Vitamin B-6 0.4mg, Vitamin E 2.59mg, Vitamin K 307.1µg, Calcium 181mg, Iron 3.51mg

Minerals: Copper 0.371mg, Magnesium 109mg, Phosphorus 162mg, Selenium 1.8µg, Zinc 1.21mg

33. Morning Breakfast

There is nothing more refreshing than an energy drink in the morning. By trying it on a daily basis, you increase your stamina and weight loss much faster than if you take it once a month. That is because of the high content of fiber and nutrients. "Morning Breakfast" is also very low in calories, and contains turmeric root which is a very good anti-inflammatory, and one of nature's great healers.

- Apple: Contains natural laxative
- Carrot: Do wonders for boosting the immune system
- Celery: Calms the nerve because of high calcium content
- Ginger root: Lowers the LDL cholesterol
- Lemon: Great for health problems because it contains potassium
- Pears: Have anti-oxidants that help prevent high blood pressure
- Turmeric root: Has powerful anti-inflammatory effects

Ingredients:

- Apples - 2 medium 360g

- Carrots - 3 medium 180g
- Celery - 3 stalks, large 190g
- Ginger Root - 1 thumb 22g
- Lemons (peeled) - 2 fruits 165g
- Pears - 2 medium 355g
- Turmeric Root - 6 thumbs 140g

How to prepare:

- **Wash all the ingredients. Peel if necessary.**
- **Juice them all together for a great drink.**

Total calories: 364

Vitamins: Vitamin A 1107µg, Vitamin C 283.1mg, Vitamin B-6 1.025mg, Vitamin E 2mg, Vitamin K 73.6µg, Calcium 191mg, Iron 3.41mg

Minerals: Copper 0.743mg, Magnesium 115mg, Phosphorus 212mg, Selenium 1.5µg, Zinc 1.35mg

34. Start Healthy

Sweet potatoes are full of potassium and calcium which are important for everyone, no matter what your lifestyle. "Start Healthy" is rich in vitamins and minerals. Try this drink about 30-60 minutes before eating, to allow your body to absorb all the nutrients from fruits and vegetables first.

- Apples: Reduce risk of cancer
- Beetroots: Cleanse the colon and strengthen the liver
- Carrot: Beta-carotene lowers risk of muscular degeneration
- Orange: Stimulates white cells to fight infection
- Pepper: Has antioxidant and antibacterial effects
- Sweet Potato: Helps the immune system get stronger

Ingredients:

- Apples (golden delicious) - 2 medium 360g
- Beetroots - 2 beets 160g
- Carrot - 1 large 70g
- Orange (optional) - 1 fruit 135g
- Pepper (sweet red) - 1 medium 115g

- Sweet Potato – 130g

How to prepare:

- **Wash all the ingredients. Peel if necessary.**
- **Juice them all together for a great drink.**

Total calories: 250

Vitamins: Vitamin A 1211µg, Vitamin C 177.5mg, Vitamin B-6 0.735mg, Vitamin E 2.51mg, Vitamin K 18.1µg, Calcium 118mg, Iron 2.31mg

Minerals: Copper 0.35mg, Magnesium 85mg, Phosphorus 167mg, Selenium 1.8µg, Zinc 1.15mg

35. Natural Mix

Juices have always been a delicious drink, but they are more than just that, they are a fountain of health and, if made properly with the right ingredients, they can provide all the vitamins your body needs. This is a great juice recipe that has weight loss effects and helps the immune system build up. You should drink it in the morning or in the evening after dinner. Let's see what great effects it will have on your own body.

- Apple: Contains boron, for bones strength

- Celery: Has nutrients that protect the eyes and prevent age-related degeneration of vision

- Cucumber: Great source of silicon that improves health of the skin

- Dandelion Greens: help reduce stress and reduce cancer

- Kale: Provides a large nutritional punch with few calorie count

- Lemon: Helps increase weight loss

Ingredients:

- Apples - 2 medium 360g

- Celery - 2 stalks, medium 80g

- Cucumber - 1/2 cucumber 150g

- Dandelion Greens - 1 cup, chopped 55g

- Kale - 3 leaves 105g

- Lemon - 1/2 fruit 42g

How to prepare:

- **Wash all the ingredients. Peel if necessary.**

- **Juice them all together for a great drink.**

Total calories: 165

Vitamins: Vitamin A 581µg, Vitamin C 133.2mg, Vitamin B-6 0.504mg, Vitamin E 2mg, Vitamin K 854µg, Calcium 238mg, Iron 3.13mg

Minerals: Copper 1.29mg, Magnesium 81mg, Phosphorus 163mg, Selenium 1.4µg, Zinc 0.95mg

36. Surprise Juice

Weight loss has always been associated with juice recipes, because they have few calories, and the nutrients get absorbed faster by your body. It should be consumed within 30-60 minutes before a meal, and the effects should be felt only after a week or so. Here are some great benefits of this juice that for sure will improve your health condition.

- Apple: Protects brain cells from free radical damage
- Carrot: Consumption of beta-carotene has been linked to reduce risk of several cancers
- Cilantro: Reduces the amount of damaged fats in the cell membranes
- Collard Green: Rich in source of nutrients with anti-cancer properties
- Kale: Contains sulforaphane that helps support a healthy immune system
- Pepper: Has antioxidant abilities so it can neutralize free radicals in the body

Ingredients:

- Apple - 1 medium 180g

- Carrots - 3 medium 180g

- Cilantro - 1 handful 35g

- Collard Greens - 1 cup, chopped 35g

- Kale - 4 leaves (8-12") 140g

- Pepper (sweet red) - 1 medium 115g

How to prepare:

- **Wash all the ingredients. Peel if necessary.**

- **Juice them all together for a great drink.**

Total calories: 158

Vitamins: Vitamin A 1832µg, Vitamin C 252.1mg, Vitamin B-6 0.812mg, Vitamin E 3.52mg, Vitamin K 898.1µg, Calcium 275mg, Iron 2.86mg

Minerals: Copper 1.61mg, Magnesium 90mg, Phosphorus 187mg, Selenium 1.6µg, Zinc 1.28mg

37. Broccoli Combo

"Broccoli Combo" is simple to prepare, you should drink it in the morning so you can charge yourself with energy for the rest of the day. If you can have it every two days, it will be even more beneficial. It has a high percentage of vitamin C that will make your immune system stronger and give you strength to fight any health problems.

- Broccoli : Is high on iron, which is an important nutrient to ensure energy levels stay high

- Cabbage: Helps detoxify the body and keeps blood pressure from getting high

- Kale: Helps in proper functioning of insulin and regulates blood sugar

Ingredients:

- Broccoli - 1 stalk 150g

- Cabbage - 1/2 head, medium 450g

- Kale - 4 leaves (8-12") 140g

How to prepare:

- **Wash all the ingredients. Peel if necessary.**

- **Juice them all together for a great drink.**

Total calories: 117

Vitamins: Vitamin A 536μg, Vitamin C 328.1mg, Vitamin B-6 0.841mg, Vitamin E 1mg, Vitamin K 1038.6μg, Calcium 321mg, Iron 3.68mg

Minerals: Copper 1.571mg, Magnesium 102mg, Phosphorus 241mg, Selenium 4.3μg, Zinc 1.41mg

38. Tropical Ginger

If you plan on having a healthy diet and losing some weight, then this juice recipe should be on the menu as well. "Tropical Ginger" is full of vitamins and nutrients that will not only benefit your body, but will also increase your energy levels throughout the day. For this recipe you will need the listed ingredients and you should enjoy the juice in the evening.

- Ginger Root: Prevents cancerous tumor growth, and can help knock out a fever

- Kale: Is a rich source of organosulfur compounds that fight many cancers

- Mango: Contains enzymes that help in breaking down protein

- Orange: Contains hesperidin that lowers high blood pressure

- Pineapple: Decreases risk of progression of age-related muscular degeneration

Ingredients:

- Ginger Root - 1/2 thumb 10g

- Kale - 4 leaves (8-12") 140g

- Mango - 1 fruit without refuse 335g

- Orange - 1 small 95g

- Pineapple - 1 cup, chunks 165g

How to prepare:

- **Wash all the ingredients. Peel if necessary.**

- **Juice them all together for a great drink.**

Total calories: 231

Vitamins: Vitamin A 625µg, Vitamin C 294.2mg, Vitamin B-6 0.725mg, Vitamin E 2.24mg, Vitamin K 701.2µg, Calcium 215mg, Iron 2.25mg

Minerals: Copper 1.904mg, Magnesium 93mg, Phosphorus 143mg, Selenium 2.5µg, Zinc 0.95mg

39. Lemon King

Juice recipes are a healthy and modern way of staying fit to making sure your body gets all the important nutrients, minerals and vitamins it needs. It is best to have this juice in the morning, or you can also replace a daily snack with it. If you drink this juice on a daily basis you will feel the effects in your body and in your mind as well.

- Apple: Reduces cholesterol and decreases risk of diabetes
- Celery: Regulates the body's alkaline balance
- Kale: Helps support a healthy immune system and has anti-cancer properties
- Lemon: prevents problems related to skin
- Spinach: Great to lower blood pressure, and cleans out the system by removing accumulated wastes

Ingredients:

- Apples (granny smith) - 4 medium 725g
- Celery - 3 stalks, large 190g
- Kale - 2 leaves (8-12") 70g
- Lemon (peeled) - 1 fruit 58g

- Spinach - 4 cups 120g

How to prepare:

- Wash all the ingredients. Peal if necessary.
- Juice them all together for a great drink.

Total calories: 254

Vitamins: Vitamin A 679µg, Vitamin C 131.4mg, Vitamin B-6 0.627mg, Vitamin E 3.03mg, Vitamin K 801.2µg, Calcium 251mg, Iron 4.11mg

Minerals: Copper 1.041mg, Magnesium 131mg, Phosphorus 180mg, Selenium 2µg, Zinc 1.10mg

40. Huge Mix

One of the best methods to lose weight and drop fat is by starting the day off with this delicious juice. Bell peppers help increase our body's metabolism by lowering triglycerides which are stored in our body, and this helps burn calories more effectively. Here are other benefits from this juice recipe:

- Cayenne Pepper : Blocks transmission of pain, so it can help relieve the pain to a certain degree

- Celery : Reduces high blood pressure

- Cilantro: Is very low in calories and contains no cholesterol

- Garlic : Reduces blood triglycerides and reduces arterial plaque formation

- Onion : For centuries, onions have been used to reduce inflammation and heal infections

- Tomato : Has anti-oxidant properties and improves the digestive function

Ingredients:

- Cayenne Pepper (spice) 0.20g

- Celery - 1 stalk, large 63g

- Cilantro - 1 handful 35g

- Garlic - 1 clove 3g

- Onion (spring/scallion) - 1 medium 14g

- Pepper (sweet green) - 1 medium 115g

- Salt (himalayan) - 1 dash 0.2g

- Tomato - 1 cup cherry tomatoes 145g

How to prepare:

- **Wash all the ingredients. Peel if necessary.**

- **Juice them all together for a great drink.**

Total calories: 35

Vitamins: Vitamin A 156µg, Vitamin C 91.5mg, Vitamin B-6 0.370mg, Vitamin E 1.65mg, Vitamin K 122.2µg, Calcium 63mg, Iron 1.25mg

Minerals: Copper 0.200mg, Magnesium 33mg, Phosphorus 70mg, Selenium 0.7µg, Zinc 0.52mg

41. Granny Juice

If you are a juice lover, here is a great recipe for you. It will help improve your body's metabolism and increase weight loss. It is best to be served in the morning or within 30 to 60 minutes before having a meal or you can easily replace a snack with it. This juice has a high content of potassium and phosphorous, which helps release the symptoms of stress. So if you are having a bad day, you can always relax and enjoy this drink, it will help. Here are some other great effects of this recipe:

- Apple: Great source of fiber without too many calories

- Carrot: Very rich in vitamin A, good for improving eyesight

- Cucumber: Relieves bad breath and rehydrates body

- Grapes: Reduce cells ability to store fat by about 130 percent, significantly assisting in weight loss

- Pepper: Stimulates white cells to fight infection, naturally building a good immune system

- Spinach: High alkalinity properties make it perfect choice for people suffering inflammatory ailments, like osteoarthritis

- Tomato: Improves heart health by helping lower blood pressure

Ingredients:

- Apples (green) - 2 medium 355g
- Carrots - 3 medium 180g
- Cucumber - 1 cucumber 300g
- Grapes (green) - 15 grapes 90g
- Pepper (sweet green) - 1 medium 115g
- Spinach - 2 cups 60g
- Tomato - 1 medium whole 115g

How to prepare:

- **Wash all the ingredients. Peel if necessary.**
- **Juice them all together for a great drink.**

Total calories: 221

Vitamins: Vitamin A 1325µg, Vitamin C 114.2mg, Vitamin B-6 0.701mg, Vitamin E 2.79mg, Vitamin K 270.1µg, Calcium 171mg, Iron 2.9mg

Minerals: Copper 0.429mg, Magnesium 112mg, Phosphorus 185mg, Selenium 1.1mg, Zinc 1.31mg

42. Mineral Fountain

No matter what kind of lifestyle you have, you should make time for a healthy juice that can be an excellent source of minerals and vitamins. If you want to lose weight, improve your health, or just feel better, a natural juice can do that for you. It's a true friend when it comes down to improving the way your body looks, works and feels, and the outcome will definitely be a positive one. Here are the benefits of this juice recipe.

- Apple: One apple per day reduces risk of breast cancer by 16 percent

- Beetroot: Very healing for liver toxicity or bile ailments such as food poisoning, hepatitis

- Ginger Root: Reduces inflammation and inhibits replication of the herpes simplex virus

- Lemon: Adding lemon juice will help increase weight loss

- Pineapple: Helps combat the formation of free radicals known to cause cancer

Ingredients:

- Apple - 1 medium 180g

- Beetroot (golden) - 1 beet 80g

- Ginger Root - 1 thumb 24g
- Lemon - 1/2 fruit 29g
- Pineapple - 2 slices 332g
- Pumpkin Pie Spice (a dash) - 1/4 tsp 0.42g

How to prepare:

- **Wash all the ingredients. Peel if necessary.**
- **Juice them all together for a great drink.**

Total calories: 179

Vitamins: Vitamin A 11μg, Vitamin C 121.4mg, Vitamin B-6 0.385mg, Vitamin E 0.35mg, Vitamin K 4.5μg, Calcium 55mg, Iron 1.53mg

Minerals: Copper 0.36mg, Magnesium 56mg, Phosphorus 64mg, Selenium 0.8μg, Zinc 0.60mg

43. Health Friend

Here is a great and easy to make juice recipe that will give you incredible weight loss results and helping you get all the necessary nutrients your body needs. It's a great way to saving time and will maximize your day. You can easily replace an unhealthy snack with this juice. Here are the effects from this juice:

- Asparagus: Contains potassium that is known for reducing fat, and it's also low in natural sodium and has no cholesterol, which helps when trying to lose weight

- Celery: Has high antioxidant content, and has an antibacterial effect against Salmonella

- Cilantro: Is a natural water purifier, and a vital nutrient that is required for formation and maintenance of strong bones

Ingredients:

- Asparagus - 6 spears, medium 95g
- Celery - 3 stalks, large 185g
- Cilantro - 1 handful 32g

How to prepare:

- Wash all the ingredients. Peel if necessary.

- Juice them all together for a great drink.

Total calories: 20

Vitamins: Vitamin A 131µg, Vitamin C 14.2mg, Vitamin B-6 0.185mg, Vitamin E 1.63mg, Vitamin K 139.1µg, Calcium 84mg, Iron 2.09mg

Minerals: Copper 0.218mg, Magnesium 28mg, Phosphorus 75mg, Selenium 2.1µg, Zinc 0.63mg

44. Sweet Juice

You will have fun making this juice recipe, it's easy to prepare and all the ingredients are delightful. So let's get started, try to serve this juice at least 30 to 60 minutes before eating your next meal. "Sweet Juice" is a great way to accelerate weight loss and improve your health at the same time. If you are ready, let's review some of the benefits that will come from this recipe.

- Beetroot: High in carbohydrates which means it is a great instant energy source, and useful in helping metabolize fat

- Carrot: Has a cleaning action on the liver and lowers the cholesterol levels

- Sweet Potato: Contains anti-inflammatory nutrients

Ingredients:

- Beetroot - 1 beet 80g

- Carrots - 3 medium 181g

- Sweet Potato - 1/2 63g

How to prepare:

- **Wash all the ingredients. Peel if necessary.**

- **Juice them all together for a great drink.**

Total calories: 85

Vitamins: Vitamin A 1386µg, Vitamin C 11.2mg, Vitamin B-6 0.30mg, Vitamin E 0.92mg, Vitamin K 17.4µg, Calcium 63mg, Iron 1.10mg

Minerals: Copper 0.165mg, Magnesium 39mg, Phosphorus 87mg, Selenium 0.7µg, Zinc 0.61mg

45. Pure Life

Bring this healthy juice recipe into your life, the effects will change your weight problems in a positive way and make your body stronger. You can drink it any time of the day; just make sure you do it 30 to 60 minutes before having a meal. Ok, so let's see now what this juice has to offer for you.

- Bitter Melon: Contains a chemical that acts like insulin to help reduce blood sugar levels

- Grapefruit: Works as an excellent appetite suppressant and also beneficial in the treatment of fatigue

- Lemon: Assists in curing respiratory problems, and helps increasing weight loss

Ingredients:

- Bitter Melon - 1 bitter melon 120g

- Grapefruit - 1/2 large 165g

- Lemon (with peel) - 1 fruit 80g

How to prepare:

- **Wash all the ingredients. Peel if necessary.**

- **Juice them all together for a great drink.**

Total calories: 45

Vitamins: Vitamin A 73µg, Vitamin C 142mg, Vitamin B-6 0.131mg, Vitamin E 0.23mg, Folate 80µg, Calcium 45mg, Iron 0.81mg

Minerals: Copper 0.102mg, Magnesium 27mg, Phosphorus 43mg, Selenium 0.7µg, Zinc 0.80mg

46. Vitamin Time

We all want to be healthy, but most of the time we forget that we have to act responsibly to do this. Juice recipes are an excellent way to solve this problem. A couple of minutes a day and you get a big flow of vitamins and minerals. "Vitamin Time" fits the description and let's see what it has to offer.

- Apple: Contains pectin that lowers cholesterol
- Carrot: Eliminates excess fluids from the body and reduces stroke risk
- Ginger Root: Helps digesting fatty foods and breaks down proteins, helping in reducing weight
- Lemon: Inhibits the development of cancer, and increases weight loss

Ingredients:

- Apple - 1 medium 180g
- Carrots - 8 medium 485g
- Ginger Root - 1 thumb 22g
- Lemon - 1 fruit 82g

How to prepare:

- Wash all the ingredients. Peel if necessary.
- Juice them all together for a great drink.

Total calories: 165

Vitamins: Vitamin A 2851µg, Vitamin C 56mg, Vitamin B-6 0.589mg, Vitamin E 2.50mg, Vitamin K 46.8µg, Calcium 132mg, Iron 1.61mg

Minerals: Copper 0.242mg, Magnesium 58mg, Phosphorus 145mg, Selenium 0.6µg, Zinc 0.94mg

47. Tasty ABC

This juice recipe is best to be served in the morning because it is a great way to give your body an energy boost, and it will also keep your mind focused and active for the rest of the day. If you were looking for something to help you with the benefits mentioned above, or just looking for that recipe that helps reducing fat, you should try this one. Here are some other benefits it has to offer.

- Apple: Boosts the immune system and helps detoxify your liver

- Beetroot: Lowers blood pressure, very rich in fiber and is a great source of betaine, a nutrient that helps protects cells

- Carrots: Prevent heart disease and cleanse the body

Ingredients:

- Apple - 1 medium 180g

- Beet Root - 1 beet 80g

- Carrots - 2 large 141g

How to prepare:

- **Wash all the ingredients. Peel if necessary.**

- **Juice them all together for a great drink.**

Total calories: 95

Vitamins: Vitamin A 837µg. Vitamin C 13.5mg, Vitamin B-6 0.21mg, Vitamin E 0.88mg, Vitamin K 16.1µg, Calcium 49mg, Iron 0.90mg

Minerals: Copper 0.121mg, Magnesium 31mg, Phosphorus 71mg, Selenium 0.4µg, Zinc 0.47mg

48. Delight in Three

"Delight in Three" is a simple juice recipe that can be served to the entire family, just make sure you do it 30 to 60 minutes before having a meal. Feel free to try it and see the results; it's going to bring only positive things into your life, for your health and the way your body look. Let's see how to prepare it and what it will provide.

- Apple: Increases bone density, boosts the immune system and reduces cholesterol

- Beetroot: Regenerates and reactivates the red blood cells and supplies fresh oxygen to the body

- Sweet Potato: Plays an important role in our energy levels, moods, heart, nerves, skin, and teeth.

Ingredients:

- Apples - 2 medium 360g

- Beet Root - 1 beet 80g

- Sweet Potato - 135g

How to prepare:

- **Wash all the ingredients. Peel if necessary.**

- **Juice them all together for a great drink.**

Total calories: 175

Vitamins: Vitamin A 643µg, Vitamin C 16.5mg, Vitamin B-6 0.331mg, Vitamin E 0.71mg, Vitamin K 7.3µg, Calcium 51mg, Iron 1.31mg

Minerals: Copper 0.247mg, Magnesium 48mg, Phosphorus 92mg, Selenium 0.8µg, Zinc 0.56mg

49. Evening Flavor

No more excuses when it comes to losing weight. "Evening Flavor" is a great juice recipe that's perfect for the job. You should drink it in the morning to get the most of it for the rest of the day. It won't take more than 5 minutes to prepare, and for those 5 minutes you will get awesome results! Check out what is waiting for you.

- Beetroot:
- Carrot:
- Celery:
- Cucumber:
- Pear:
- Ginger Root:

Ingredients:

- Beetroot (golden) - 1 beet 80g
- Carrots - 3 large 215g
- Celery - 4 stalks, large 255g
- Cucumber - 1/2 cucumber 150g
- Ginger Root - 1/2 thumb 11g

- Pear (bosc) - 1 medium 174g

How to prepare:

- **Wash all the ingredients. Peel if necessary.**
- **Juice them all together for a great drink.**

Total calories: 147

Vitamins: Vitamin A 1304µg, Vitamin C 25mg, Vitamin B-6 0.462mg, Vitamin E 1.66mg, Vitamin K 1.82mg, Calcium 158mg, Iron 1.73mg

Minerals: Copper 0.334mg, Magnesium 75mg, Phosphorus 161mg, Selenium 1.7µg, Zinc 1.15mg

50. Vegetable Time

Here is a great juice recipe that you must try. If you are on a diet or want to have a healthier body, it will help. It's easy to prepare and you should drink it in the morning as an extra snack. The ingredients are high on important nutrients and very low on calories, so it will help you accelerate your progress. Let's see what benefits await you with this recipe.

- **Beetroots:** They fight inflammation and lower your blood pressure
- **Carrots:** Great source of beta-carotene that reduces risk of cancer
- **Celery:** Reduces cholesterol and regulates your alkaline balance
- **Parsley:** Excellent blood purifier and builder
- **Pepper:** Has antibacterial and antioxidant effects
- **Radishes:** Great way to satisfy hunger and keep a low caloric intake
- **Tomatoes:** The fiber, potassium, vitamin C and choline content in tomatoes all support heart health

Ingredients:

- Beetroot - 1 beet 81g
- Carrots - 2 medium 121g
- Celery - 2 stalks, large 125g
- Parsley - 4 handful 160g
- Pepper (jalapeno) (seeds/ribs removed) - 1 pepper 13g
- Radishes - 12 medium 50g
- Tomatoes - 4 plum tomatoes 246g

How to prepare:

- **Wash all the ingredients. Peel if necessary.**
- **Juice them all together for a great drink.**

Total calories: 100

Vitamins: Vitamin A 1273µg, Vitamin C 200.4mg, Vitamin B-6 0.51mg, Vitamin E 2.92mg, Vitamin K 1890.3µg, Calcium 254mg, Iron 8.45mg

Minerals: Copper 0.403mg, Magnesium 113mg, Phosphorus 190mg, Selenium 1.1µg, Zinc 2.11mg

OTHER GREAT TITLES BY THIS AUTHOR

50 Weight Loss Juice Recipes for Body Cleansing: Lose Weight Fast Before Your Wedding, Party, or Special Event

50 Juice Recipes to Lower Your Blood Pressure: An Easy Way to Reduce High Blood Pressure

35 Diabetic Meal Recipes: The Most Delicious Way to Stay Healthy

www.ingramcontent.com/pod-product-compliance
Lightning Source LLC
Chambersburg PA
CBHW070125080526
44586CB00015B/1556